John Chuckman is the former chief economist for Texaco, Canada, and now teaches economics part-time. He left Chicago and the USA as a young man, in opposition to the Vietnam War, and still lives in Canada today. He is a regular columnist for a number of on-line publications, and has also written for Toronto's *Globe and Mail*, the *Washington Post*, and the *Chicago Tribune*.

What's It All About?

The Decline of the American Empire

Heavyweight issues, lightweight read

John Chuckman

Magpie Books, London

Marjorie

Constable & Robinson Ltd
3 The Lanchesters
162 Fulham Palace Road
London W6 9ER

This edition published by Magpie Books,
an imprint of Constable & Robinson Ltd 2007

A copy of the British Library Cataloguing in Publication Data
is available from the British Library

ISBN-13: 978-1-84529-625-4
ISBN-10: 1-84529-625-7

Printed and bound in the European Union

1 3 5 7 9 10 8 6 4 2

Contents

Introduction

A Great Epoch

The decline of the American empire and the rise of China and India are in many respects separate topics, but they are related in important and illuminating ways. Examining them together tells us a great deal about the fundamental nature of economic growth, its effect upon national political and social institutions, and the whole great web of international relationships which those institutions form.

One of the great epochs of history is now underway, bringing a set of changes to the world's society undoubtedly greater than any previously experienced. One likes to avoid using the expression "greater than any," but here it is appropriate because it is not just the scale of the changes, affecting as they do the entire world and the nature of international relationships, it is humanity's way of regarding itself and the world that is changing, something fundamental and far-reaching in its consequences. The proximate cause of this phenomenon is globalization, although the everyday connotations of that almost clichéd word don't begin to capture the complexity of its implications.

Great epochs certainly have occurred before, and, considering the conditions of ongoing change that characterize the entire Modern Era since the Middle Ages, it is not easy to explain why any particular set of changes should stand out in people's perceptions and memories. We tend to explain this by the idea of revolutions, not political revolutions, but industrial revolutions or electronic revolutions or social revolutions, although it seems clear that economic and social revolutions always feature in the events leading to great political upheavals. The decline of the American empire and the rise of two great new states, China and India, plus a number of other significant, although lesser, economic powers might be called a geopolitical revolution. Does that mean we face great political upheavals ahead? It is a distinct possibility.

It is not hard to see how the decades following the dawn of globalization may well be troubled and extremely unsettling as local customs, habits, laws, and even languages come under great stress from huge and rapid economic changes. The stresses of negotiating and adjusting to comprehensive trade agreements, disagreements over what is fair, disagreements over currencies, disagreements over pollution, the stress of rising prices for important commodities, expectations generally of still greater change, shifts in the economic and military importance of various nations, and growing recognition of the need for better global regulation of many matters going in the face of parochial, "go it alone" attitudes like those displayed by the USA in recent years will be just some of the certain difficulties ahead. Sweeping changes in the world's pattern of trade, in the generation and distribution of economic wealth, international competition in the search for secure resources, and the rise and fall of great corporate entities will alter the daily lives and expectations of many, many millions of the world's inhabitants.

While the author does not forecast revolutions, civil wars, trade wars, and great human migrations coming out of changes over the next several decades, it is not at all unrealistic to anticipate just such events, much as the Industrial Revolution or English Enclosures generated many social and political upheavals on the smaller scales of their time. One fervently hopes the promise of globalization for a better world where greater numbers enjoy more prosperous lives, where human creativity better flourishes, where democratic values and human rights gain broader support, and where the world is less under the influence of a single, arbitrary, and unquestioned power will not be extinguished by upheavals wrought of the very same change.

Chapter One

The Astonishing Rise of the Chinese Economy

Quite apart from the adjustments and difficulties implicit in the new age of globalization, the history of great powers rising itself seems always fraught with troubling events. China does very much want to be a great power, and it feels entitled to that status in the world by virtue of many claims: its four thousand years of history; its great cultural achievements; the sheer mass of its population, representing a fifth of the planet; its past humiliations by Western nations; awareness of its people's talents; and now one of the most astonishing economic rises in modern history. But it is crucial to understand that China has been very clear that it wishes to enjoy a peaceful rise to power, and the single greatest question facing the world over the next quarter century is truly whether the USA will allow this to happen peacefully.

China enjoys the extraordinary situation of sharing its border with fifteen other countries, and it is at peace with all of them. It has been involved in no great conflict for half a century. America's record over the same period is virtually the polar opposite of China's, having been involved in almost constant colonial wars, and the Chinese correctly see America's attitude towards them as crucial. The Chinese perceive an American network of containment around them, including South Korea, Taiwan, and Japan, all places having treaties or bases or special relationships with the United States. Some Chinese actually see it as part of their great task to peacefully guide the United States in its imperial decline, a remarkable way of looking at the situation, and a view which better than any example I can think of catches an important and exceptional quality of the Chinese mind.

However, even if one chooses to be a pessimist about the next several decades, the lessons of history and economics give us every reason to be optimistic about the very long term. Humanity has suffered many setbacks just since coming out of the Middle Ages, and yet it has ultimately made real, measurable progress. Science, which really is another word for knowledge, truly is beginning to reign over many aspects of human affairs, sweeping away the shadows of superstition and prejudice and the unwarranted powers they have always supported. Globalization, and all the many adjustments it entails is humanity's fate, and China will inevitably, even if there are conflicts ahead, take its place as a great power.

I say measurable progress because whatever socio-economic standard we choose, those nations heavily influenced by the advance of science are better off than they were a few decades ago and immensely better off than they were a few centuries ago. This is true of human life expectancy, infant mortality, average level of education, the availability of arts and cultural institutions, and many others important, measurable variables.

Despite being run by a party whose original tenets are anything but scientific, China under the Communist Party has strongly embraced science. China is doing science and technical work in a number of areas at or near the frontiers of knowledge. Its infrastructure for technology and communications is growing at an astonishing pace. According to the

World Health Organization, average life expectancy in China has grown from 35 years in the 1950s to 71 in 2003. These are nothing less than amazing achievements for a nation which still accurately often describes itself as developing.

China has become the world's second largest economy and is expected to become the largest in less than twenty-five years, but statistics sometimes can muddle our understanding as much as they clarify it. When China does become the world's largest economy, life for the average Chinese citizen will still be at a considerably lower standard than life in Europe or America. China's wealth will not be sufficient to threaten the United States, nor has China ever indicated it intends in any way to threaten the United States. China's ambitions appear entirely reasonable: to develop its people and resources in a peaceful way without the shadow of American imperial interests cast across its territory.

Dramatic statements about China challenging the United States are not to be found in this book, although it has a lot to say about what is happening in China and its effects upon the relative position of America. Assuming, as there is every reason to assume, China continues along its current path of development, it will be a different world in a couple of decades. The relative decline of the American Empire will not be owing solely to the rise of China and other newly vigorous economies, a far more robust India, South Korea, Vietnam, Brazil, Russia, and others, however. There are serious internal problems in the United States itself. A multi-polar world is emerging. This represents not only economic challenge to the United States, but more certainly a challenge to its recent, easy imperial privileges. In the sophisticated sphere of managing its affairs sensibly so as not to damage the delicate workings of a world in transition, it represents a great and certain challenge to the United States, a nation which frequently has acted in headstrong and destructive ways when confronted by external challenge.

Of course, the rise of new economic powers is not the only change on the horizon. New ways of doing things and new technologies which have contributed to globalization will have many other important effects. Because change builds on change, the rate of change in advanced society now grows the way compound interest grows. This means that change itself is well on its way towards becoming the single great reality of human affairs. Someday, perhaps we will cease speaking of epochs and revolutions, but for now, I think the concept remains valid, and it is clear we are over the threshold of a great new one.

It seems, at first reading, a contradictory idea but change itself has been the main connecting thread through history. Change forges links between old, familiar things and new things that will become old and familiar to the current generation, but the pace of change in human society was originally so slow it could barely be perceived, much as an effort to watch a seed sprouting and becoming a plant. Despite periodic setbacks like wars and dark ages of superstition, the rate of economic and social change has accelerated to the point where it is noticeable in many aspects not just in a lifetime but in a period of a decade or less. Likely, over no considerable time, the ability to perceive significant change will shorten to months and eventually even briefer periods. Short of thermonuclear war or earth's collision with a comet, I think it reasonable to say there is no moving backward along this curve of socioeconomic change the slope of which seems to grow only steeper (the slope of a curve measures the rate or pace at which whatever is graphed changes, a vertically steep curve indicating rapid change).

The change with which we are concerned is not that represented by a fall fashion show or next year's automobile models. While these examples may well contain occasionally bits of significant change in technology, generally they represent the kind of relatively small change marketing and popular media bill and coo over for all of a few weeks. I am referring to change that changes the way we do all or most things, sometimes even the way we perceive the world, the kind we associate with technologies such as radio, the transistor, the personal computer, the Internet, commercial flight, automobiles in general, electricity, satellites, or genetics. It is not an exaggeration to describe the change represented by these developments as revolutionary or, at least, potentially revolutionary, for rarely do such things come in a revolutionary form first time out but do represent new, extraordinarily fruitful concepts that will continue being developed and perfected for years into more practical things, affecting the lives and livelihoods of millions of people.

At the most basic level, the driving force in society-changing phenomena is the discovery and application of technology. As we shall see, once technologies are practical and applied, it is always associated with immediate economic change, and, in the wake of economic change, come social and political changes. It's as though a whole sequence of change comes embedded or implicit in any really useful thing or concept, almost the way a huge tree with all of its seasonal variations and fruits is implicit in a tiny seed.

Consider an interesting astronomical analogy for the changes underway in the world. For centuries, astronomers observed and recorded occasional great, brilliant events in the night sky. It is only comparatively recently that science established that these events are exploding stars, novas and super-novas, which are part of the basic, ongoing operation of the universe. And it is only very recently that science has learned these titanic events serve as thermonuclear factories, creating complex substances and hurling them to the far reaches of space. Some of these substances are mixed or fused with others in interstellar space, forming still others. These complex substances include organic compounds that may well provide the seeds for life as they arrive at countless distant planets and large moons.

The nature of globalization, a new economic state or era born out of many dramatic technological advances, their various effects intermingling and interacting after being hurled across the globe, and the changes it implies are key themes of this book. The rise of China, India, and others represent special cases of globalization, and here I advise readers that the limits of the author's experience and knowledge make the case of China feature here heavily. This reflects years of personal interest, the experience of having taught many Chinese students in freshman economics, and the experience of our family providing the "home-stay" for a bright Chinese student who did half of his high school in Canada and is now distinguishing himself at the author's alma mater, the University of Toronto.

To some extent, the emphasis may be justified by the fact that, so far, it is China that is having a huge impact on international arrangements and particularly on the relative status of the United States in the world. There is little doubt that India will also play an important role, but at this time it is well behind China, and the structure of its economic transformation is different to China's, China's representing more closely the historic pattern of most advanced nations' course of development. Each of these countries, as we shall see, has a different set of advantages and disadvantages in its quest for advancement. We cannot predict accurately where the complex changes underway will take us over the long term, that is strictly the subject of science fiction, but we can safely say that many things we take for granted today in international relationships are going to change and change more quickly than many suspect.

Economic growth always has been a revolutionary force, careful historical analysis revealing it as the great triggering-force of revolutions in human affairs, unforgiving and powerful in dissolving away human traditions and institutions, and yet it remains underestimated by many who think in terms of social movements or political agendas as main driving forces. But it is economic change that causes people to live longer lives, to alter the number of children they have, to put away old customs, to change their traditional ways of dress, and even to alter their speech, old accents fading and parochial modes of speech being left behind and even languages themselves gradually altering in response to new needs and emphases. One of the great consequences of economic growth not widely understood is change in the very forms of government: as it turns out, economic growth really is the parent of modern democratic values and advances in human rights.

The concept of creative destruction in economics, a term coined by economist Joseph Schumpeter, although intended to apply to the deaths of established firms and industries over time, nicely describes this broader phenomenon associated with all economic development. With increasing rates of change, and those occurring on a global scale, we may say that creative destruction very much will become humanity's common experience, eventually an easily observable event for most. The fact that economic growth is now occurring at a rapid pace across vast new stretches of the planet certainly does have some resemblance to the effects of an exploding star. The seeds for new forms of economic, social, and political life surely have been spread irretrievably around the globe.

One of the major technological changes contributing to globalization, but with implications going far beyond our experience of it thus far, is the planet's literally becoming "wired," the creation of a network comparable in many respects to a world brain and nervous system of ever-increasing complexity. That network is already important in world trade, but its capabilities over a number of decades will increase dramatically. New software, hardware, materials, and procedures being developed almost constantly are generating what we might view as a kind of evolution in a non-living thing towards something that more and more will function almost as a living system tying together distant parts of the planet in ways far more dramatic than jet travel.

There are periodic hints suggesting where we might be headed, an outstanding example being the numerous science projects now underway using thousands of individual personal computers all over the world running the same program to provide experimenters' investigation something like occasional supercomputer capacity. Just one of many on-going applications of this approach is the immense number-crunching going on night and day in the search for extraterrestrial, intelligent radio communications by sorting through oceans of naturally-occurring signals generated by stars.

There is also the "wiki" approach to designing projects, as in the on-line, free encyclopedia called *Wikipedia*, the word *wiki* being Hawaiian for *fast*. Wiki-documents are collective creations easily altered either by anyone reading them on his or her own computer or by any of a specified group of participants. In China, outstanding motorcycles are being designed by a group of interested designers working together in a wiki-project while living in different places.

The eventual complexity and robustness of the world electronic nervous system, with many paths to achieving the same goal, should mean that no nation or corporation will be able to control it. This system will evolve now continuously, not just extending the reach and interaction of human intelligence but extending also even the human senses – sight, sound, and touch will effectively be extended in their reach to anywhere on the planet where an appropriate sensor and communications exist. It will be possible for the world's best people in almost any field to examine and analyze the same observations and data simultaneously, whether from under the oceans or from another planet. Inventions and new industries are increasingly in the virtual world, from information services to programs that assist or do almost anything we can imagine, and it is important to keep in mind that anything in the virtual world is by its nature globalized.

I think of the example of major newspapers on the Internet. At first, many created limited sites merely feeling the need to "be there." Increasingly, over just a small number of years, these sites have become quite sophisticated and, sometimes with their many links, more interesting than the original newspapers themselves. It does seem clear now, and I would not have accepted this proposition only a decade ago, that virtual newspapers will soon replace paper ones in much of the world.

But the virtual newspapers already do more than begin to replace paper ones. Read any major broadsheet on the Internet, and you will find through readers' comments on stories (an increasingly common feature in the best papers), the kinds of advertising contained, the way editors and writers address their readers, and even subtle changes in language usage (particularly noticeable in British papers) that the very nature of the newspaper is changing before our eyes. The switch from paper to pixels is only part of the change, although that allows for incalculably many new ways of doing things. The audiences and markets for all major newspapers, the things that truly define newspapers and their purposes, have become far larger and more complex in a very short time.

There was a time in Europe, only about five hundred years ago, when few people went beyond their own villages, and when they did do so, it was a modest effort, perhaps only to attend a regional fair. Roads were terrible or did not exist, the roads that existed were often toll-roads, transportation by horse or wagon was slow, uncomfortable, and costly, rivers often had no bridges, for the most part there was no equivalent of modern signage telling you where to turn to reach a certain destination, and many restrictions existed between regions of what we now think of as the same country, including sometimes the levying of taxes for entering or leaving.

Chapter Two

Technological Innovation and Globalization

Trade and markets may be said to have started when people previously self-sufficient in some rudimentary fashion began to specialize in their various tasks and exchange them with others. This exchange made everyone participating better off because it allowed the individuals best suited to produce each kind of good or service - owing to innate skills or experience or aptitude - to do so and thereby increased total production of all of them. Specialization generated a surplus to a village's need for some products, and this surplus could be traded in neighboring villages for still other products. The trade between villages created additional specialization and generated still greater surpluses, creating an incentive for trade further afield and, in turn, powerful incentives to improve the technology of travel.

Of course, actual historical events are never quite so neat or straightforward as events in such an illustrative story, but the story nevertheless captures fundamental economic truths and something like the sequence of events marks the embryonic beginning of what we now call globalization.

The birth of the Modern Era, the history of Europe since coming out of the Middle Ages, is one of step-by-step change in economic arrangements, induced each step of the way by changes in technology, often fairly simple and seemingly inconsequential changes in technology. What seem in hindsight simple developments – an improved plow, a stronger horse, or a new approach to fertilizing fields – ended by making considerable change in economic arrangements as they worked their way through regions and, eventually, countries.

The dispersion of new techniques or tools was itself slow for the same reasons that extensive travel was uncommon. There were, of course, no telephones or telegraphs. There was no regular mail service until well into the nineteenth century. There were private mail systems using stage riders, but these were mainly for the use of great lords. Most people were illiterate anyway since education had costs few could bear and offered few potential economic advantages for those living so simple a life in such a relatively unchanging society. Church and state made provision for education to a very few, generally the exceptionally talented or powerful (although surprisingly large numbers of the aristocracy spurned education themselves in favor of hunting and hawking – there are many historical references to the plodding ignorance of great lords), recognizing the need for talented clerks, scribes, advisers, and translators.

With each new set of economic arrangements, still further technological change produced still more change in economic arrangements. There was a countless number of modest improvements: an improved hoe or shovel, a better way to weave cloth, reasonably efficient wheels and wagon suspensions, improved saddles, or the use of new crop varieties. Travel across countries, too, gradually improved, leading to a greater flow of new ideas and techniques across regions and countries.

We speak of stages or steps, but these technological and concomitant economic changes are best understood as flows, sometimes trickling, at other times more turbulent, rather than discrete events. Of course, much as with modern physics' conception of energy as both wave and particle, they may perhaps be conceived of as both flows and series of discrete, small events.

There were particularly notable periods when various flows came together to produce experiences we characterize as revolutions or new epochs. The opening of the great age of exploration by sailing ships was certainly one of these. It had huge effects on societies and their economies, including the discovery of important new plants such as potatoes, tomatoes, corn, coffee, tobacco, and various fruits. It vastly expanded the areas of the sea that could be commercially fished. Whole new industries were created by the needs for ship building, ship design, ship repair, putting up provisions, developing new preservation techniques, introducing new plants into European agriculture, experimenting with the characteristics of new plants, introducing new foods into the diets of millions, and so on. Eventually, some discoveries from the New World were to become not just agricultural staples but distinguishing marks of European cultures – as tomatoes for Italy or potatoes for Ireland – despite their only having been known a few hundred years.

The Enclosures in England – the fencing or hedging of fields that had previously been left open during the Middle Ages for local peasants to pasture their animals – was another of these revolutionary experiences. Enclosures, with its move away from common fields with sets of elaborate, medieval rules for shared use to private, fenced-in properties that generated new wealth through more efficient animal husbandry for the exclusive benefit of the property owners – almost perfectly symbolize the beginning of transition from the Late Middle Ages to the Modern Era. Many village and country situations that had been stable, quiet, seemingly sleepy and unchanging for centuries started to change dramatically.

The Enclosures brought many unpleasant side-effects, including a notable increase in wandering beggars, thievery, and the burden for villages of having to support impoverished peasants, but then all events we characterize as revolutions or new epochs come with much harshness and unhappiness. It is interesting to note that the Enclosures were often viewed as evil, anti-social, and selfish. The Tudors fought them. Leaders from Cardinal Wolsey under Henry VIII to Elizabeth I worked to suppress them or at least alleviate their impact, passing laws in the interests of disenfranchised peasants, including laws for the poor that marked in some respects the beginnings of the modern welfare state. But all efforts to actually suppress Enclosures were unsuccessful as the underlying changes in economics were unstoppable and continued to exercise their enormous and inexorable influence on the activities of those who owned property.

Perhaps the most famous such historical experience was the Industrial Revolution which we typically associate with late eighteenth-century England, although there were the beginnings of factories, the harnessing of water power, and certain kinds of machines in the time of Henry VIII and before in a number of European countries. The Industrial Revolution is famous for filling cities with desperate, job-seeking migrants from the country, filling previously clean air with smoke and filth, mangling countless operators of early machines, setting children to work on just such machines, and generally increasing noise and crime and seeming disorder. What is happening now in China and, to a lesser extent, India is a repeat of the English Industrial Revolution of more than two centuries ago, only the demands driving these Asian industrial revolutions and the materials and supplies being transformed into products come from every part of the planet.

Education becoming available to most of society, at least at an elementary level, marked another great transforming experience. From society's point of view, access to education provided a mechanism for identifying and elevating the most talented. As economies grew in the eighteenth and nineteenth centuries, an increasingly large pool of talented people was needed for a wide variety of managerial tasks. Formal education, a form of what economists call investment in human capital, provided a pool of able, highly flexible people who could move from one important task to another in increasingly complex and specialized economies. It also provided most of the population with rudimentary levels of literacy and calculation skills becoming increasingly necessary in more complex industrial jobs with more sophisticated machines, and it provided the foundation for training skilled trades which had begun to develop in response to ever more complex machines and buildings. The very nature of what was being taught also changed – university education in the late Middle Ages had focused heavily on theology, canon law, and the languages of scripture.

Now that the world has, for the first time, a large, permanent establishment of highly educated people dedicated to science and research, who have budgets of tens of billions of dollars per year, technological change comes much more rapidly. And each wave of change builds on what has come before. As Sir Isaac Newton said, with regard to his own remarkable discoveries, "If I have seen farther it is by standing on the shoulders of giants," a reference to his predecessors, such as Galileo. In fact, technological and economic changes have become unavoidable, and if certain inventions and discoveries are not made by one group in a certain year, they will almost certainly be made by another group in another year. In recent times, many ideas or innovations have come almost simultaneously from more than one source.

Yes, there are still geniuses with unique talents, but there are so many people and so many dedicated and clever ones, that the concept of the lone genius doing what no one else can do is starting to recede into the mists of time. In the ancient world with its small population, education was hard to come by and recognized geniuses were rare. Individual original thinkers stood out in a way that is far less likely to occur in the future.

I think of the fascinating discovery recently of the operation of the Antikythera Mechanism from ancient Greece – a remarkable object composed of gears, discovered in the Mediterranean, encrusted with sediment, about a hundred years ago, but not understood until scrutiny with modern technology revealed its secrets. It is a shoe box-size analogue computer, more than two thousand years old, that can generate calendars and predict eclipses. Nothing like it would exist, so far as we know, for another thousand years or more. The workmanship and design are comparable with those of early European clocks.

But it is not really a mystery why such amazing technology in the ancient world seemed to come to such a dead end. The knowledge and skills that went into creating such a machine at that time were limited to a few, fragile human beings in each generation, and in the ages of war, barbarism, and religious fanaticism which were to come, how easily such knowledge was lost. You have only to reflect on the death of Archimedes, one of the greatest scientific geniuses of the ancient world, who was killed by a Roman soldier during the sack of Syracuse.

When the Dark Ages descended on Europe, faith and superstition replaced incentives for advance and human understanding. Even in the Dark Ages there were clever tinkerers, but they risked censure, punishment, or even death if their work was widely shared, and it is virtually impossible for science to develop without the sharing of discoveries. The final emergence of the Renaissance came out of re-discovering ancient texts and the painfully slow accumulation of new ideas and ways of thinking against the inertia of Church authorities and the princes supported by them in their absolute power. The Middle Ages' divine right of kings represented a symbiotic arrangement in which great ecclesiastical and temporal aristocrats reinforced each other's authority. In fact, discoveries from ancient texts showed Renaissance scholars that the Church had sometimes misrepresented matters in its translations and adopted traditions, starting the undercurrent that would before long swell to become the Reformation, still another revolutionary experience.

I like to think of China's period under Mao being comparable to Europe's period of rule by Catholicism and its loyal princes. Both Christianity and Communism are religious faiths, and both are served by some very fervent and anti-intellectual servants. Maoism was like a fundamentalist offshoot of Communism, and the viciousness of some of its practices led to the relatively short life of modern China's Dark Ages. The Chinese have largely returned to their ancient, pragmatic, hard-working ways, with respect for knowledge and ability again ranking highly. Examine the Chinese in all the many lands to which they have migrated, and you will find people who create businesses or who become scholars, scientists, or financial experts. As a people, they have a strong endowment of mathematical reasoning skills and are natural entrepreneurs, and Maoism went against many of their natural inclinations.

Although technological and economic change, as now established in the modern world, is virtually unstoppable, every once in a while, groups similar to the Luddites – workers in early nineteenth-century England who smashed machines out of fear of losing their traditional jobs – appear, but their efforts are doomed to fail, just as the Tudor monarchs could not stop the Enclosures. Luddites come in many forms with many different fears and superstitions, from the fascists and Nazis of the 1930s to the anti-globalization crowds that mob every meeting of the G8 today, but they are all doomed in a modern science-driven economy to fail or to succeed only for a comparatively short time. This is one of the blessings of advancing science and one of the many ways economic change is related to political change.

In ages dominated by religion or ancient tradition, it was difficult for the scientific process to embed itself in society, and there were various sputterings and false starts, but once society is adequately permeated with the process of technological and economic change, there really is no going back. The underlying force of these changes derives from the basic human desire to understand the universe and to harness its forces for benefit, and this desire doesn't go away and cannot be long suppressed. Religion itself, one of humanity's most enduring institutions, was undoubtedly born far back in the mists of time at least in part out of the same powerful desire. The difference now from the ages dominated by religious faith is that science and technology actually deliver these benefits to a remarkable extent so that everyone can experience them, a bit like the rarely-occurring miracles of religion, only these new miracles are able to be repeated over and over without limit, and they come with the promise of still more miracles.

Economic change, despite its destructive side-effects, benefits too many people, and there are just too many people in too many places now dedicated full-time to its promotion for it to suffer long-term reversal. And so, too, the social changes generated by technological and economic change. There is no escaping it. Even if you live in one of the most remote parts of the globe, the impact of this change will only be slowed, not eliminated. Some Inuit hunters still use dogs to pull their sledges, but many now buzz around on snowmobiles, and when you have snowmobiles, you need places to buy gasoline, repair shops, and so on. Because you can travel further, faster on a snowmobile, you may feel the need for communications and safety equipment never used before. Modern clothing engineered against the cold will begin replacing traditional clothing made from animal hides. You will also increasingly be drawn into the society from which these things come.

I think of the culture and values of the Old South in the United States, often regarded as quaint or charming, but, in fact, brutal and primitive in many respects, not just in racial matters, including violent and vindictive attitudes about honor, respect, and family not all that different from what we find in some of the world's economic backwaters. These values were well preserved long after the American Civil War, certainly into the 1930s, when, in parts of the South, families still gathered for Sunday picnics where the chief attraction was a public lynching. The values were preserved because the American South was itself an economic backwater, showing no great growth and no great diversification away from its largely rural economy for a long period.

People think real change in the South's abusive practices came with the civil rights movement, and to a limited extent this is true. The basis for permanent change, however, came as American manufacturers started leaving their old centres in the East and Midwest, moving to what became known as the Sun Belt for the attractions of lower taxes, a pool of poor labor with low salary expectations, little or no unionization, and local governments very friendly to their interests. The fresh air of economic growth started flowing through many former backwaters. New faces with new attitudes showed up in increasing numbers to manage these establishments and to serve the needs of a new class in the Old South. People living there moved for opportunities in the new establishments, and local education was improved in many cases to respond to the new demands. Dark corners started to recede, and today attitudes in the South are much changed.

We even see to some extent the fading of the lolling, thick-tongued accents that characterized the South, such accents anywhere always reflecting long periods of lack of mobility, new people, and new ideas. I remember hearing stories from British friends that also testify to the way even accents can change. Young people moving to London in the postwar period from the country or small towns with traditional heavy accents often took elocution lessons, a la Professor Henry Higgins in *My Fair Lady*, to learn to speak with more of what we think of as a BBC accent. Schools offering such services became common in London by the 1970s.

In China, the long-established color of good luck and happiness is red. That is why there is so much red used in Chinese decorations, why the Communist party adopted the color red for its symbols, and why brides traditionally wear the color red on their wedding days. Yet today, in the part of China officially designated as the New Economic Zone, the part of China that is advancing at breath-taking speed, brides now often get married dressed in white gowns just as they do in North America; white in the old Chinese culture was the color of mourning. Some would say this represents only a shallow mimicking of Western styles, and there is some truth in that, but at the deepest level, it truly represents the power of rapid economic growth to generate social, cultural, and other changes.

When once, just several hundred years ago, people in Europe expected to live virtually the same, generally short, life in the same place as their fathers or mothers (exactly what we observed only a couple of decades ago in India or China and still observe in parts of the developing world), today people in advanced countries automatically expect changes, cures, fixes, new discoveries, and movement almost without limit. No one expects to do what his or her parents did; the social implications of this change on its own has been revolutionary in traditional societies. As soon as some new threat emerges - HIV/AIDS, for example - people in advanced societies now expect, or even demand, a cure. This marks a true revolution in human thinking, encompassing far more and of greater day-to-day importance than, say, the Copernican revolution which placed the sun at the centre of the planets rather than the earth.

People in advanced countries today have no idea where their careers will take them. Their movement represents a kind of constant seeding and re-seeding of ideas and practices, somewhat in the fashion of the way inter-stellar material is thought to have seeded the early earth with important organic compounds. People in these places may land up in another part of the country or of the world. And if they do land up far from home, they will be able to travel back home, and they will be able to communicate easily as often as they wish. This way of experiencing the world is also new to humans.

Globalization is just a name for what began happening in European villages hundreds of years ago, but is now happening across the entire planet. It is the largest of a series of concentric circles - ripples in a pond, if you will - flowing out from different-sized pebbles being tossed into the water, lapping now at most of the planet from the first tiny ripples that affected a few villages. The technologies of fast shipping and travel, excellent communications, and computers doing immensely complex tasks have put the residents of any town with these assets in direct competition with the residents of advanced places. A furniture maker in China now competes directly with a furniture maker in Minnesota or Italy for the first time in history.

The emergence of globalized competition is comparable to the changes that first began putting the residents of different towns or villages into competition with each other, except that the scale of everything involved is now immensely greater. Scale is important in science and economics. The scale of things not only changes efficiencies, it fundamentally alters the nature of things. Compare the nature of a family's subsistence-level farm to a giant corporate farm or a home pie-baking business to an industrial bakery. It is not just that big operations produce immense quantities of products, but in doing so, each task and tool is different. Chinese manufacturers are being scaled to serve the world, and their competitors abroad have all been merging in recent decades to form global-sized firms.

The furniture maker in China has workers available in almost limitless numbers and each at a tiny fraction of the cost of workers in Minnesota or Italy, but it is not fair and completely lacking in perspective to say the Chinese furniture maker is exploiting workers because their wages are so low compared to those in advanced societies. You might just as reasonably say that American workers in non-defence industries are exploited because their wages are lower than the workers in defence plants or that reporters at the *Podunk News* are exploited compared to those ensconced in princely fashion at the *New York Times*.

The costs of living are very different across societies and locations within societies – a number of American corporations actually have schedules of different wages for the same job in various locations – as are the nature of things people consider essential to sustaining their lives. There is also the important fact of different perspectives: new factory workers in China and other places previously had only the option of grinding village poverty with almost no prospect for change. Not that shabby exploitation doesn't exist, for it certainly does even in places like New York City, it's just that *exploitation* does not come close to describing the general situation.

The work former Chinese peasants now do is often unpleasant and dirty, but then so was the work of the Industrial Revolution, indeed far more so. Going through this transition is an unavoidable step in economic development, much as the disturbing changes experienced by peasants during the English Enclosures. The new workers now earn cash, many for the first time, and can anticipate moving on to better jobs or accumulating a tiny bit of capital to start a business of their own. For the first time in centuries for many, their children can expect to do something different, and perhaps better, than their parents.

Chapter Three

Pollution

Many people in North America or Europe have lost any sense of perspective in their relative affluence. Village life in really poor places is not only hard, dirty, and with little to inspire the imagination, it generally does not even include the convenience of money. The immense flexibility we take for granted every working day of receiving reliable cash for our labors is missing from the lives of many. The few bits of money that previously found their way into villages were hoarded like treasure. So the opportunity to work for cash wages can come as something of a godsend, and, if you are like the Chinese who typically have as many members of a family working as they can to accumulate for the family's benefit, otherwise unpleasant factories may look like fine things indeed.

A common attack made on Chinese industry today from America, one of many attacks on China from that source, is that its growing economy is dirty and polluting. And that is true, but it is an incomplete truth because it contains no perspective. How many Americans remember the river in Cleveland, emptying into Lake Erie, that actually caught fire a few decades ago, so polluted was it with hydrocarbons? How many remember the huge asbestos industry, still roaring long into the 1960s, mining and manufacturing a wide range of toxic products that killed tens of thousands over time and contaminated countless buildings still standing today? How many remember America's early military efforts with atomic energy when atmospheric tests were conducted within sight of Las Vegas? How many people today remember the great killer fogs of London? One of these in the 1950s killed several thousand Londoners. These, as it turned out, weren't fogs at all – the romantic, atmospheric stuff of Sherlock Holmes movies – but smog, especially filthy with the smoke of millions of coal-burning hearths.

Chinese authorities are well aware of the problems of pollution – after all, they have a couple of hundred years of Western experience to study in addition to their own recent experience – but many efforts so far, including specific multi-year plans for reductions, have been notable failures. Local choices for quick growth have not favored controlling pollutants. There has been little progress, but the problems are being studied with research into many technologies such as relatively clean-burning coal. No sudden cures are going to appear for the smoggy air and chemically-stained rivers, but recent information published in China, unquestionably with the approval of the Communist Party, suggests that the way is being prepared for a new effort. Under China's system, only a serious effort by national authorities, one with penalties for violators, is likely to achieve results, but then that fact is no different for the United States whose most important pollution laws and regulatory agencies are national. The technology available to China in its industrial revolution to fight pollution is more sophisticated than what was available before in the West, and I would be very surprised if no progress is made in the near future.

China has substantial reserves of coal and, as one would expect, uses the resource that it has for its development. Coal was also the fuel which drove industrial development in England, Germany, and the United States. Following the pattern of development in these countries, the next stage of development for China is likely to see oil replacing coal for many uses. It was as recently as my childhood in Chicago during the 1950s that many of the thousands of old apartment buildings were converted from coal heating to oil heating. I used to see the coal deliveries in the alleys as a boy, and I remember some of the conversion projects which were interesting events for a young urban child. Western environmentalists may find it difficult to credit because people in advanced countries have a difficult time not thinking anachronistically about such matters, but the historical move from coal to oil is an important one for a cleaner environment. Yet China has little oil, and the United States is not likely to facilitate its gaining access to reserves abroad. So competition and conflict in the search for secure reserves abroad seem destined to be part of future international relations, although it is in the world's best interest from an environmental point of view that China does gain such access.

In the year 2000, China adopted the first level of the European Union's emission standards for automobiles, Euro I, and it has now adopted Euro IV as its standard, with effect from 2010. That represents a huge change in one decade and a far faster response to the emissions problem than the record of the United States. Of course, since China is hoping to export a lot of cars in the future, it must accommodate the needs of foreign markets. Some far-thinking ideas are taking hold in China, an example being a goal to make the new, revitalized Shanghai the world's first city where vehicles run only on hydrogen. This is a remarkable commitment for a country like China. Of course, it also reflects the awareness of Chinese scientists, engineers, and planners that "green" technologies are going to be in great demand throughout the advanced world before very long. China will, in environmental matters as in other areas of technology, certainly become a world innovation leader.

The patience engendered by countless centuries of horse-like peasant toil certainly leaves people in China and India equipped to tolerate many excesses of their own industrial revolutions. Also, at least in many large plants, conditions are not at all as gruesome as they were in the days when English workers, many of them children, were chained to machines in factories dimly lit with oil-lamps. Simple mistakes with crude and unforgiving machinery frequently claimed lives or limbs, and there was no insurance or pensions or medical care to speak of.

It is important to understand the economic principle that all workers are not equal. Education, natural abilities, aptitudes, health, and cultural attitudes – things that go into the concepts of endowments of, and investments in, human capital – make some workers more equal than other workers. Generally speaking, healthy workers are more productive than unhealthy ones, educated ones more productive than uneducated ones, and so those with greater natural abilities compared to those with less. Thus, in some cases, workers in the West can still comfortably compete with those in Beijing or Mumbai because their productivity is higher through both societal and private investments in health and education.

Workers in the West also use superior tools in many industries. The quality or sophistication of a tool directly affects the productivity of the person using it (how much output you get for each worker in the case of labor productivity, the most usual measure of productivity), as when two pilots on a jet airliner equipped with the latest computerization do the same job as three pilots – pilot, co-pilot, and navigator – on a previous generation of jet airliner. Of course, what a country like China does in economic terms is substitute its plentiful labor for its scarce capital (not just money, but the economists' term for tools and machines used in production). This is an entirely rational, economic decision, but the productivity of each worker is necessarily lower when he or she is not using the same tool as workers in another place. This, however, is not an important consideration when you are in the early stages of national growth and when you have the supply of labor China has. Differences in productivity are also important to explaining differences in wages.

But the situation is constantly changing. As Chinese families gain income, they invest in the education and health of their children. This parental impulse is even more keenly felt under China's one-child policy intended to limit population growth (by the way, this policy is more flexible than many Westerners realize because families may pay fines to have more children, which is exactly what some of the new middle class do). The government, too, invests in children through new schools and clinics. From 1986, the provision of public education in China increased from five to nine years. That may not sound like a lot, but it is greater than what is provided in many other parts of the world, and the quality of those nine years may well be greater than the average for the United States in terms of academic rigour. As Chinese entrepreneurs earn money, they invest in better tools and facilities. The Chinese are great savers, and their ancient habits are powerful mechanisms for future growth.

China's economic take-off may be said to have begun with the de-collectivization of agriculture in the late 1970s and early 1980s under Deng Xiaoping. Over just a few years, many of the immense inefficiencies of collectivized agriculture were swept away in a series of epochal events. While agriculture still does not take place on privately-owned plots (the Chinese government continues to grapple ideologically with the concept of private property), the new arrangements went a long way in that direction and saw many families return to tending farms in the way that their ancestors had once done. The surpluses generated from a transition to more economically efficient agriculture helped finance many investments under reforms which also brought more economic rationality to industry. In 2007, China's economy will have grown about nine-fold in fewer than three decades. That is the power of compound growth at high annual rates.

At the phenomenal 9–10 per cent rates of growth China has experienced recently (10 per cent average over 2003–2005), the economy doubles in size every eight to seven years. It doesn't take many doublings before one arrives at astronomical numbers for national output (to convince yourself, try doubling even a small number repeatedly), but it is in the nature of economics to be unable to sustain such rates of growth indefinitely. In the very nature of things, high rates of growth are easier over a low base, or starting, figure than they are over a large one. Doubling output from one unit to two is very different from doubling output from one trillion to two trillion. The Chinese certainly understand this, and they fully expect their rates of growth to slow: the eleventh five-year plan (2006–2010) projects annual average growth of 7.5 per cent, but no one can reasonably say just when Chinese growth will fall to anything near the range of 2–4 per cent that we view as normal in Western countries (rates which take from thirty-five to fewer than eighteen years for the size of an economy to double once).

We think of China as a communist nation, but China's private economy currently comprises about two-thirds of its national economy. This is a proportion within the experience of Western countries, being about the same as that of the United Kingdom in the 1980s. If expected growth trends hold, China's economy will become equal in size to that of the United States in less than a quarter of a century, around the year 2030. However, at that time the average per capita income in China would still be only a quarter of that in the United States (although it would be substantially greater than the current level of about one-twenty-fifth of the per capita income in the United States).

Averages are needed for comparisons, but they tend to blur hard realities. Over very different things, averages are always deceptive, as in the proverbial story of a person with one hand in hot water and one hand in ice water being on average warm. National income averages blur great differences within populations. This is as true for an advanced country like the United States as it is for China. Despite a high per capita income for the USA, something like 12 per cent of the American population has an income below the poverty line. In China this figure is about 10 per cent, although that implies a very large absolute number applied to a population of 1.3 billion.

All this is to say, that high-growth economies imply considerable inequalities. Various portions of economic systems resemble pressure or temperature gradients in physics in which energy moves across the gradient precisely because of differences from high to low, thus creating a flow. In a free economy, income tends to concentrate in relatively few hands, those with aggressive instincts, the extremely hard working, and the cunning. The accumulation of income in economic terms serves the purpose of concentrating capital needed for investment, a key component to growth. Across the economic spectrum of any economy, there are those with less and less success at, or focus on, accumulating capital. At the extreme end of the economic spectrum are those who do not compete successfully and fail to accumulate capital: the weak, the disabled, and those lacking in aggression and cunning.

Social Darwinism was coined as a pejorative term intended to attack those who would like to see economies unfettered by restrictions or regulations, allowing the strong to flourish and the weak to be reduced to misery or simply to perish. In its extreme form, a completely free economy might be represented by the brutal operation of an organization like the Mafia in a relatively poor population such as that of a small town in Sicily. No modern state works in quite this way, not even the United States which has perhaps the strongest inclination in this direction. In any advanced state, some portion of each person's income, usually a higher proportion for those with higher incomes, is taken in tax from those who are successful at accumulating to be redistributed as support for the less successfully competitive. Taking too much slows the growth of an economy; taking too little increases misery within a society. Getting that balance right, in circumstances which are always changing, is the basis of the perennial political conflict between conservative and liberal or progressive parties in a democratic society. In an enlightened society, redistribution of some portion of income isn't just a charitable measure, it is intended to avoid the severe social consequences of immense inequality. Social instability, in the absence of repressive force by the state, arises almost automatically where there are great inequalities.

In China, over recent years, things have been moving in the opposite direction with many of the traditional (communist) social measures having been gradually reduced or removed: guaranteed jobs in factories or collectivized farms (often called the "iron rice bowl" in the West) and free health care being key examples. I would have expected the difference in the standard of living between the eastern, coastal area of the New Economic Zone and large portions of traditionally poor western China to have become pronounced by now, but I have heard from people who have traveled in western China that the cities there are also showing signs of a new prosperity. There will still be pressures to move from rural to urban areas, as people did in nineteenth-century Europe and America, but in today's China the number of potential migrants is far greater and therefore potentially more disruptive to orderly development. Control of these pressures is one of the arguments for authoritarian government in the early stages of economic development. The government of China, despite having gradually dropped many of the practices and policies of communism, still controls internal migration and closely monitors and clamps down on political and social movements which threaten to fragment the state.

The Chinese government's well-publicized opposition to the Falun Gong movement is a good example of this. Falun Gong is a vaguely religious, social and quasi-political movement – a sort of Chinese version of a Californian New Age movement. It is not too far-fetched to imagine that the Falun Gong receives financial assistance from US intelligence agencies as a way of generating internal difficulties for the Chinese state and embarrassing its government. Repressive action against the Falun Gong features regularly in the American media as a way of representing the limitations on personal freedoms in China. This is not widely understood in the West, but freedom of religion exists in contemporary China, and people openly attend various houses of worship. The only exception to this freedom are religious organizations which oppose the government or aspects of its policies, and that is the reason for the ban on Falun Gong which is as much a political movement as a religious one. The Chinese government also insists on making its own appointments of bishops for the Catholic Church, ignoring the choices of the Vatican, but this is no different from the practice in Europe centuries ago – the Vatican was constantly fighting with various European princes over the appointment of bishops.

The Chinese government uses its police and army to suppress numerous public protests, although there is no evidence of widespread demands for political reform in China or of the existence of national political links between incidents of local unrest. The extent and importance of these disturbances, considering China's gigantic population and its many significant and diverse problems, may well be exaggerated by some analysts. To put things in perspective it is worth remembering how often police and troops have been used in the United States to quell protests, often with considerable violence. First World War veterans, for example, marching on Washington to call for the bonuses which had been promised to them were baton-charged by mounted troops, while unionized workers in the 1930s were regularly beaten and shot at by the police, and the National Guard has often been used to put down black protests in US cities, often with extreme violence.

There have been huge internal migrations in China as the demand for skills and labour brought about by the nation's explosive economic growth draws people from rural areas. China maintains a residence registration system under which all citizens are associated with particular places and are generally divided into urban and rural categories. This allows the government to control movement into the cities. It does not mean that all migrants are absolutely excluded from cities, rather that their status there often resembles that of guest workers in parts of Europe in the recent past or Mexican agricultural workers in the United States or black South Africans under apartheid. This is not an attractive form of regulation in an advanced society, but it is hard to see it as anything other than indispensable in a country of China's immense size and widespread poverty. The movements of population that occurred during the Industrial Revolution and during the nineteenth century would seem very limited compared with what would happen in China in the absence of any such restrictions. The completely free movement of the population would create almost insurmountable difficulties in the orderly development of urban areas. The consequences of such unfettered free movement are to be seen in many parts of the world where cities grow at breakneck speed and extreme squalor and high levels of crime result. This has been true for Mexico City and also for a number of large South American cities.

The results of just a few decades of change in China are already to be seen all over the world. In China itself – mainly in that portion of China designated by the government as the New Economic Zone, a rip-roaring capitalist economy in all but name – the change is breathtaking. China's new rich drive Mercedes and BMWs. China has become the third largest market for Rolls-Royce cars. Successful Chinese now often build Western-style homes on land they may not technically own but lease long-term. Apartment blocks, some luxurious even by Western standards, are thrown up monthly. Huge areas of Shanghai and Beijing have been torn down and rebuilt, in much the same way as the centre of Berlin has been dramatically rebuilt. Transportation and communication systems are growing at staggering speeds. During 2006, the number of Chinese using the Internet is reported to have grown by 30 per cent, to reach more than 130 million (this compares to a few more than 200 million Internet users in America and about 300 million in Europe, both of which enjoy far greater average wealth), an amazing number for what many still think of as a third-world country. More than 50 million Chinese have high-speed connections. Asia as a whole now has more Internet users, nearly 400 million, than any other continent.

When one reflects on some of the stories of the Cultural Revolution, as revealed in books such as *Wild Swans*, these changes are dizzying, occurring as they have done during the lifespan of someone who could even now be regarded as only middle-aged. During the Cultural Revolution, students were sent in great numbers to the countryside or to factories to help out and to imbibe, and be humbled by, the views and attitudes of peasants and workers. The students were frequently shocked by their experiences, learning for the first time how backward much of China was, discovering, for example, that many peasants lived in primitive huts or even, literally, in caves.

Today, on streets where Mao saw clouds of state-manufactured bicycles scudding by, there are traffic jams as dense and unpleasant as anything found in North America or Europe. China develops its infrastructure at a rate equal to that of adding the city of Toronto each month. China now has more than 400 million mobile telephone users as well as levels of service in some areas way in advance of those in the West. For example, a request to an Internet service provider to get connected in China will see a company technician arrive at your door virtually straight away to do the necessary set-up work.

Chapter Four

Made in China: the World's Factory

Just a few decades ago, very few Chinese goods were sold in North America and Europe. Now, whether it's clothes, furniture, light fixtures, or tools that you're buying, they are more likely than not to bear the imprint "Made in China". These goods are not the sort of cheap and flimsy stuff we came to expect from immediately post-war Japan – goods typified by paper cocktail umbrellas or gumball-machine prizes. In short, many years ago "Made in Japan" used to mean cheap, tinny, without substance, but, before long, Japan's excellent quality cameras, cars, watches, and machine tools changed that connotation entirely. "Made in Japan" quickly came to mean "quality", so much so that traditional industries of long standing, such as the German camera industry and the US television-manufacturing industry collapsed in the face of Japanese competitors. Chinese goods today are quality goods, often as good, if not better, than anyone else has ever made, at often remarkable prices. As one beaming Chinese student told me, "China make everything."

And this is only the beginning. In a few years, China will be competing in the world market with products such as cars and their relative cost and high quality will make these products irresistible. Already Chinese cars are being road-tested in America, but those familiar with the industry in China expect that it will be at least five years before there is any real assault on the US market. The USA will almost certainly respond with protectionist measures when this anticipated assault materializes. United States politicians have developed a mantra about being free traders who must nevertheless respond to predatory behaviour by unfair traders abroad. Almost all such talk is nonsense used to disguise protectionism.

It is an interesting to speculate here whether major American manufacturers, who already have interests in China and whose American plants are among the most financially-troubled in the world, will eventually base much of their production in China. One can recall the attitudes of US workers only a few decades ago reflected in contemptuous talk about foreign cars, meaning especially Japanese cars. Today Japanese cars are just part of the landscape, large numbers of them made in US plants. Imagine a reversal of fortune that sees many or most "US" cars made in China. That is precisely what we see already with the products of many other well-known US brands, even prestigious designer fashion labels. At the time of writing, Chrysler, a company in some trouble owing to the changing pattern of demand with rising oil prices and a reliance on large vehicles, has indicated that it will have small cars manufactured in China and imported into North America.

The example of Japan is a highly instructive one. Near the end of the Second World War, US war planners were struggling to identify significant targets in Japan for bomber crews; all the primary targets had been flattened, as had most of the secondary targets. Japan was a wasteland, and yet, within a few decades, it was booming and competing in some sophisticated product markets. The example supports the idea that motivated, skilled people are the *sine qua non* of rapid economic growth, just the kind of asset that China possesses in abundance. It also shows how quickly arrangements and institutions can change under the influence of rapid growth: hundreds of thousands of American workers now depend on Japanese companies for their jobs, just a few decades after their fathers bombed the country flat.

I am not sure that *anyone* completely understands the long period of stagnation that Japan has experienced since the early 1990s. It has certainly had a lot to do with the collapse of a huge bubble in real estate and equity values, the kind of thing that strikes any Western economy from time to time, although the size of the Japanese bubble, owing to certain structural and cultural patterns in Japan, was truly enormous. The country still requires regulatory and banking reforms that would be uncomfortable for traditional Japan: requiring Japan's large industrial combines to use stocks and bonds rather than associating with banks for their financing. Japanese banks, particularly, were badly hurt by the collapse of the real estate bubble.

Japan is also a mature industrial economy, unlikely to provide many new industrial jobs. It has an aging population, and is experiencing a corresponding decline in its working-age population. Its population as a whole is shrinking because the fertility of women in all advanced societies – the USA, Canada, the UK, France, Germany – falls to a level that does not replace the existing population, a natural human response to increased prosperity. Western countries have tended to solve this problem through migration, but Japan has never attracted many immigrants. It is a country of great cultural and ethnic uniformity (far more so than China – note the observations of the late Edwin Reischauer, a US scholar of Asia, especially on the narrow austerity of Japanese cooking compared to the bounteous variety of China, something to which this author, who loves both cuisines, can testify) whose people tend neither to emigrate nor to welcome large numbers of immigrants whose appearances and customs differ from their own.

Japan also suffered at the hands of US protectionism during the days of its greatest growth in prosperity. Americans were very upset to see cash-flush Japanese investors buying American architectural or industrial icons and continuing to outperform American manufacturers in a number of fields. The chauvinism was palpable and unpleasant. Why didn't the Japanese buy US cars? Americans asking this were totally unaware of how unsuitable US vehicles were for Japanese conditions. At the time, US automobile companies didn't even offer the Japanese right-hand-drive vehicles (the Japanese drive on the left-hand side of the road). The value of the yen and the largely one-way flow of trade were constantly being attacked by US officials who often didn't know what they were talking about, but who knew what was politically attractive in the USA. This kind of behaviour then should serve as a warning, because there are signs of the same kinds of attitudes being displayed towards China today.

The US market is such a large one – bearing in mind that the size of a market is a factor not simply of the the number of people who live in a particular country, but also of their average income – that countries deprived in one way or another of fair access to it are at a severe economic disadvantage. United States protectionists are fully aware of this and use it to full advantage for leverage in trade and other negotiations.

The structure of the USA's protectionist mechanisms is complex and sophisticated. It is time-consuming and expensive for its targets, who are designated unfair traders, and it permits American officials to apply great economic pressure against them while maintaining the air of dedication to free trade. "Unfair traders" pretty much boils down to what American politicians label exporters of low-cost products when the competition begins to have an impact in a political constituency, especially where any political damage, such as the loss of a seat, threatens.

Such low-cost products are treated as goods being dumped into the United States – "dumping" being the selling of goods abroad at less than their cost, a practice accepted as inappropriate in all trade treaties – and countervailing duties are then levied. But with great differences between the structures and circumstances of different societies, dumping is not easily proved even when it may be taking place, and often what the United States calls dumping is nothing more than competition that it cannot challenge.

The arguments for why this or that good is regarded as being dumped are as varied and fanciful as the arguments of the lawyers in US courts seeking their fortunes through lawsuits. But in all cases, even the frequent ones in which US officials lose all the decisions of international panels and tribunals ruling on such matters, the target will have been hurt by years of delay and substantial costs.

Readers should understand that while the expression "free trade" is widely used today, *genuine* free trade between nations – that is, trade with no barriers or tariffs whatsoever – is virtually unheard of. Free-trade agreements and treaties represent negotiated or administered trade, with terms and rules carefully arranged, intended to expand trade while still protecting certain interests on each side. There are many reasons for this, including the fact that while the smaller country in a free-trade agreement stands to make the greatest economic gain, the inherent specialization in production (nations each doing what they do best to increase the total quantities of all products) means some extremely wrenching social adjustments.

Extreme specialization can also leave a country with strategic vulnerabilities, either in future wars or, more generally, in a world where not everyone adheres consistently to the principles of free trade and where a country as important as the United States may in future apply economic pressure for political reasons. Even an advanced country like Japan deliberately keeps a certain percentage of particular industries going as a strategic provision, agriculture being a good example, although it is not as competitive in those industries as it is in others.

There are also important social reasons at work in such matters, too. Societies often have strong emotional and aesthetic associations with ways of life such as farming or fishing regardless of their international competitiveness. The United States and the European Union, for example, continue to pay large subsidies to their agricultural sectors largely for this reason – subsidies which have the side-effect of suppressing world prices and damaging agriculture in many poor countries. The collapse of village life in Europe and traditional family farming in America would be socially significant and highly emotional events with political consequences, but perhaps no more so than the effects upon other societies of America's frequent claims that traditional social and cultural practices are being used as disguised barriers to imports.

This confusion of cultural issues with economic trade issues plays an important role in world trade today. When is an import regulation legitimate, intended to protect sensitive aspects of a society's culture, as opposed to being used as a mere barrier to imports? We see in this conflict dramatic evidence of trade and economic growth's power to eat away at old ways and cultures. Perhaps the clearest recent example of this problem is the reluctance of Europe (which has always had particular concerns about the health-giving qualities, or otherwise, of foods, and which, decades ago, was drinking bottled spring water before Americans had even heard of it) to accept the genetically-modified agricultural products being aggressively pushed by US corporations. The USA asserts that Europe's reluctance is nothing but a barrier to perfectly good imports, but Europeans clearly have concerns relating to health and food safety. This is a complex problem, and the reality of international trade today is that barriers, various kinds of regulations and requirements, are indeed often used in place of tariffs as a way to stop or slow imports and protect local industries, but it is equally true that societies often wish to protect ways of life or traditions though their trading partners may not appreciate this.

American protectionism in the postwar period truly erupted when Japanese car makers first started to make real inroads into the American market. At a time of rising gasoline prices in the 1970s, the Japanese offered vehicles that were fuel-efficient and attractive, a combination of qualities in which Detroit seemed to have shown little interest. American officials came up with "voluntary" quotas for the Japanese car manufacturers; the incentive for Japan to agree to this was the threat of dumping charges. The Japanese agreed to import only a certain number of cars each year. Over time, Japanese manufacturers side-stepped these restrictions in two ways: first, by building plants inside the United States employing American workers; and, second, by upgrading and adding luxury features to the models they exported from Japan, thereby greatly increasing the profitability of each unit shipped.

The efficiency of the Japanese plants in America dramatically highlighted the inefficiency of US manufacturers. The upgrading of Japan's exported vehicles had the side-effect of launching the Japanese manufacturers into the high-end automobile market in America, a direct challenge to US manufacturers of luxury vehicles. This episode is a good example of the general principle in economics that no restriction on trade can be imposed without unintended costs.

Today, despite the benefits of decades of American protectionism favouring the old-line American automobile manufacturers - benefits that are effectively paid for by Americans paying higher prices for cars - these manufacturers are the very companies which face serious financial problems, and it is a distinct possibility that one or more of them may be forced out of business. The Japanese, after decades of restrictions favourable to their American competitors, are still able to produce better vehicles at lower cost, even in their American plants. Detroit's dependence on light trucks and big utility vehicles for its profits has also recently felt the impact of sustained higher oil prices. United States manufacturers have done nothing but lose market share in their own market. The case of China is likely to be even more dramatic, with costs that are likely to threaten even the Japanese home market.

Protectionists tend to look at only one side of trade imbalances such as that which exists between China and the United States. They talk of unfair trade, but US consumers benefit tremendously from an enormous selection of quality goods at reasonable prices. These are real economic gains, the equivalent of getting a pay rise. Americans are able to buy a greater variety and quantity of goods than they would otherwise be able to. And it is not just consumers who benefit – many of North America's big-box chain stores would simply go out of business without merchandise from China, and many American brand-name manufacturers are able to compete in the global market only because some or all of their manufacturing is now done in China.

Nevertheless, there are problems here. Not problems of unfairness, but problems of adjusting to change, much as were experienced during the Enclosures in Britain. The USA, in the era following the Second World War, with the collapse of former great competitors like Japan and Germany, seemed to make almost everything for everyone, and America's workers benefited directly from the this. The USA today makes fewer and fewer things that people want, and even when the name of an American company is on the label or box, the product has often been manufactured wholly or in part in China. Some US corporations are effectively becoming hollowed-out owners of brand names, marketers, and financial centres.

We have intensifying conflicts grounded in these new realities. Claims about copyright-infringement, the copying of goods like CDs and DVDs, are in the news weekly. If you know any students from China, you will know how readily available these things are and at what give-away prices. The quality is not always very good due to the way in which materials are copied, but there is a huge market for these products. Most Americans are not aware that the exactly the same thing was done in the USA throughout the nineteenth century and before: Charles Dickens, who was both fascinated and appalled by America, was angry about American publishers stealing his work. It was a common practice at the time to issue cheap new editions of works obtained from Europe and to pay the authors nothing. Everything from novels to reference works were stolen in this fashion. Some of the publishing houses doing this developed eventually into prestigious names who today would never dream of infringing copyrights.

More complex conflicts are also developing. Chinese manufacturers are steadily becoming more sophisticated in their understanding of marketing. As they master this craft, they will have less incentive to work through American corporations for understanding of, and access to, US markets. Even now, it isn't hard to find Chinese products distributed under names which resemble something from the English magazine, *Country Life*. Chinese manufacturers will inevitably copy the designs of products they now manufacture for US firms, alter or improve them, and market them directly. In effect, when American firms subcontract their manufacturing to China, there is a huge transfer of technology and human-capital improvements (in the training and knowledge of tricks of the trade that workers receive) going on, even without the defence-sensitive sub-contracting that has so worried the Pentagon.

This is natural and largely unavoidable as well as being the way things have worked throughout the history of economic development. Exactly the same thing happened in early America each time a skilled craftsman or experienced businessman immigrated from England, Germany or elsewhere. In more than a few cases, they brought with them the designs or even samples of devices which were then simply copied. Americans, following their Revolution which ended in 1781, not only stole designs and ideas from the Mother Country, it actually became a common practice in the aftermath to refuse to pay bills owing to English factors or exporters for goods previously ordered and delivered. How the passage of a little time alters people's notions of what is acceptable!

At the level of ordinary workers, the changes in global competitiveness which have affected the USA over the last few decades have resulted in wages falling in real terms, the deterioration of trade unions, and the virtual disappearance of life-time jobs with good benefits. Many US cities have been effectively hollowed out, leaving only the rusting hulks of manufacturing plants, the result not only of competition with

China but also with many other countries, such as Germany, France and Japan, which, only a few decades before, had been economic basket cases. Opportunities for American workers without professions or trades are now largely in service industries: corporate-speak for low-paid, low-benefit jobs in big-box stores and fast-food outlets.

There are service industries which pay good wages and benefits, and, with service industries being the sector of the US economy which is growing, we may expect more services to develop into more lucrative employment opportunities. But the USA is no more assured of keeping the best of these jobs than it is of keeping other high value-added industries ("value added" is the difference between the total revenue a firm receives selling what it makes and the cost of materials and services it used but did not make: in other words, profit). Many services are activities that can only be supplied locally (hair-cutting, excavating, or house-cleaning, for example), but these are not generally the service industries offering promise for the future.

The nature of services change over time as technology evolves, just as goods do. Instead of delivering post on horse-back, people drive trucks or pilot planes. The services of lamp-lighting and wig-powdering disappear, just as the manufacture of buggy whips, slide rules and abacuses declines to nothing. New services take their place, for example the service offered by computer technicians charging a high hourly rate to go to homes and businesses to solve computer problems. The same thing is true of economic resources. A century and a half ago crude oil was not a resource; it was merely black, sticky stuff that oozed from the earth. Only sixty or seventy years ago, uranium was not a resource; now it has great value. Entering, as we are, a period of great and accelerating change in technology, we can expect new goods, new services, and new resources to be defined regularly, and based on those definitions, entire new industries will be built in a matter of decades. In fact, we can also expect that the time it will take for new industries to emerge will itself become shorter and shorter.

The USA has no special gifts for adapting to and exploiting

this kind of change, which will redefine much of what we know in as little as thirty or forty years and pretty much everything we know in a hundred. Although the USA has been highly adaptable in the postwar period, there is every reason to think that any society where economic growth is vigorously underway is highly adaptable. It is a psychological phenomenon related to what happens in disaster or war: people often demonstrate the most amazing capacities to adapt quickly to a suddenly-changed situation and to improvise or innovate. Sometimes it is said that America's loose-knit culture and diversity of population make it uniquely adaptable. I do not accept this proposition as proved. Great societies have often risen on a foundation without these characteristics: Great Britain, Germany, or France come to mind. There is even some basis for believing the opposite to be true under conditions of great stress, such as that experienced during periods of vigorous economic growth or wrenching change.

The changes now under way in the world place value on an entirely new mix of skills from those which have predominated during much of the Modern Era. Physical strength, for example, is becoming an obsolete asset. Brute work was necessary on early farms, in the industries of the Industrial Revolution, and in the industries of the USA's great era of mass production in the 1950s. Even in a country like China where factory machines are not always the very latest (after all, China is using its human capital as a substitute for the economist's notion of capital, that is, the stock of machines and buildings and tools applied to production), the machines in use are far more advanced than those of the USA in the 1950s, and, increasingly, as China accumulates wealth to develop and buy capital stock, they are the very latest.

Unskilled workers with only their strength to offer are on their way to becoming obsolete. Black people with no education who migrated from the southern states of the USA during the 1930s to 1950s as a response to the mechanization of southern agriculture to get jobs as automobile or steel workers in Detroit, Chicago or Toledo (a period known as the Great Black Migration and involving the movement of about eight million people) have in many cases fared badly since global competition caused the shrinkage of those industries in America.

The ability to work in harmony is also becoming more highly valued in the West. Consider the environments in US laboratories and high-tech industries: instead of boisterous camaraderie, one finds quiet offices and "cubes" – often acres of them – forming corporate communities which place a great stress on co-operative values. It might be said that no people on earth are better suited temperamentally to co-operative work than the Chinese.

Accelerating technological and economic change increases the value of human intelligence, both increasing the demand for it while fully utilizing the available supply. This is true not just for the breakthroughs and discoveries in laboratories that keep propelling us along, but also because intelligent people are generally more flexible and better at adapting to change. The personal computer is fast approaching the status of a household appliance, comparable to the television or radio of fifty years ago, yet it still requires a significant degree of intelligence and skill to use one to any effect. This was not true of earlier appliances or machines commonly available. Up until about the 1960s, any ordinary person who was interested enough could easily learn enough about the mechanics of a car to make at least minor repairs. By the first decade of the twenty-first century, this was no longer so true as a result of the increasingly significant role played by electronics and computers in vehicles.

The rise of women in the West testifies to the importance of all these trends. In general, women do not possess the same brute strength as men, but they do possess superior co-operative and social skills, and they represent one-half (slightly more, actually, since women survive childhood in greater numbers than men) the natural endowment of intelligence. In the past this has been severely under-utilized. While movements and organizations are important in effecting great social transitions such as the entry of women into the workplace and the professions, they are temporary adaptations, varying in form from one place to another. The underlying force of economic change is what really drives social changes, making them all but unavoidable. Today, no modern society that has already employed the best of its males can possibly compete effectively without using its best females and, indeed, substituting the best females for its less-talented males.

Of course, some will say that if that is true, then China, with its strong traditional prejudice favouring male offspring, is at a serious disadvantage. But anyone who has met numbers of students from China studying abroad will see the flaw in that reasoning. While the young people naturally carry over some of the old attitudes, young Chinese women abroad behave with remarkable independence. The very fact that their families are spending huge sums to send them abroad for years of school testifies to the amazing adaptation of a traditional people in the midst of vigorous economic growth.

The US establishment's vision of the future, implicit in its behaviour and policies, has been that traditional manufacturing jobs must pass to developing countries while greater value-added, high-tech jobs, financial services, and intellectual-property rights will provide America's economic strength. This vision provides a rather bleak outlook for the USA's unskilled and semi-skilled workers, and the USA does have a large pool of such workers, school-leavers with no technical training or special skills. These workers also have much higher expectations than their counterparts in other lands to do with life-style issues such as clothes, cars, and housing, with virtually no prospect of fulfilling them legally. This may prove a serious social problem for the United States over the next few decades.

The US establishment's vision may prove a somewhat arrogant one, because competitors like China and India do not plan to do only lower value-added work, and they are uniquely gifted to succeed. The Chinese, Japanese, and Indians have an extraordinary reservoir of natural mathematical and engineering talent - every international competition or test shows this starkly - that is only now beginning to be harnessed. There is every reason to believe that over a substantial period of time, the USA will decline to a secondary role in high-tech industries, China and India each having something like three or four times the natural mathematical endowment of the USA. Their high-growth economies and emerging modern infrastructure prepare the way for the full application of this priceless talent.

America's most important internal weakness, one that has a moral dimension and certainly an economic one, is its inability to live within its means. This is reflected in many ways, from huge national imbalances of trade and payments to grotesque levels of consumer credit and even negative saving rates. United States government officials make a great deal of noise trying to blame China for their record trade deficits – roughly one-quarter of a trillion dollars annually now – but their arguments tend to be similar to US arguments about protective countervailing duties and dumping in free-trade arrangements. Those US officials simply cannot prove, and not for want of trying, that China manages its currency, the yuan, at too low a level or that it hinders the import of American goods through policies affecting things like China's savings rate, high savings rates implying lower rates of consumption and lower levels of the imports generated by consumption. The Chinese savings rate now is about one-quarter of disposable income, disposable income representing what's left after taxes, but income tax is extremely low in China, almost non-existent by Western standards. The savings rate for a traditional people like the Chinese and a people without adequate national pension schemes is always high. It will almost certainly decline one day in response to real changes in the society, but for the foreseeable future it will remain high. The one explanation for large trade imbalances that cannot be disputed is that American consumers live beyond their means.

An individual may either save or consume out of his or her disposable (after-tax) income. The importance of saving is that it funds investment in economic capital. Even a relatively small difference in saving rates between two countries can be quite telling over just a few decades. Those who have saved more will have financed a better or greater capital stock which in turn yields a new level of choice between saving and consumption in the future.

Also ignored in official US complaints and charges are the immense economic benefits US consumers receive from quality, inexpensive Chinese goods and the fact that many Chinese industries involved in offshore manufacturing for US firms are making the continued profitability and even existence of those firms possible.

Another fact ignored in official US complaints are US actions taken to limit Chinese foreign investment in the USA and elsewhere. Only recently, the Chinese were ready to make a multi-billion-dollar investment in a US oil firm which was up for sale, a perfectly rational move, but the United States government prevented the transaction with vague mutterings about national security. The American government's action represented little more than protectionism, with perhaps a generous dollop of prejudice and superstition thrown in. It is not possible to have a rational flow of capital and payments if one party arbitrarily prevents its trading partner from making acquisitions. The situation resembles someone from abroad telling you what it is you should be buying with your own money. Ordinary Chinese people, who are still poor on average compared to Americans, do not want large quantities of American consumer goods, but Chinese companies do want to make large acquisitions in the USA. This is classic, rational economics, but the USA can be seen in many ways to be trying to work against it.

By means of various pressures and restrictions, the USA burdens those countries with which it trades extensively and which bring great benefits, a strange ambiguity which is characteristic of US attitudes towards the rest of the world. These attitudes are easily exploited by politicians and industries with an interest in protectionism. They may also, unfortunately, be exploited for more hostile and dangerous actions at some point.

Because of huge, annual trade and payment flows, China has been accumulating immense reserves of US currency, which now stand at more than a trillion dollars. Substantial downward pressure on the value of the US dollar – a result of record trade deficits, profligate war spending, and monumental tax cuts – are of great concern to China and to any other country holding significant quantities of US dollars (oil exporting countries, for example, which are paid in US dollars). Should these countries rapidly deplete their holdings, the US dollar would be severely damaged and might well lose its privileged place as the world's reserve currency, leading to greater damage still. China's vice-premier has recently asserted, though offering no details of the magnitude of the intended transactions, that China will be using its dollar reserves to increase its strategic reserves of important materials and resources, including oil. Extensive activity of this kind will not only hurt the dollar, it will also push important commodity prices up.

A natural outlet for these Chinese reserves of US currency would be natural resource and industrial concerns in the USA, which would assist the Chinese in updating their capital and securing raw materials while benefiting those Americans interested in selling their companies at the best possible prices.

These immense new trade and financial flows are just one example of a powerful interdependence which has emerged in just a few decades of rapid development in China. Only three decades after the death of Mao Zedong and the arrest of the Gang of Four, China holds more than a trillion dollars in American reserves and securities. The old saying that when you owe the bank several thousand dollars, you are at the bank's mercy, but when you owe the bank several million dollars, the bank is at your mercy, has some application here.

Over the same period, US consumers have also grown dependent on China to a degree that most people do not appreciate. Were all the Chinese goods in US stores to be magically replaced by US-made ones, the standard of living of the average American would decline significantly, and a great number of national retail operations would simply collapse. There is no reason, short of some overwhelming world event or hostile US policy intervention, to expect a change in the existing trade pattern over the foreseeable future. Indeed, it is likely that the pattern will become more pronounced in the coming years.

This new interdependence has weakened US imperial power. Already, the USA is not in a position simply to demand that China make various internal adjustments to assist the USA's trade position, although a recent, very large, high-level American delegation attempted to do just that. Chinese officials undoubtedly offered powerful counter-arguments – the benefits to US industry of manufacturing in China, the cautious and responsible way in which China manages its vast dollar reserves, and the USA's inability to manage its appetites – and the US delegation left pretty much empty-handed.

There is always a danger that the United States, never very patient in international affairs, may resort to greater protectionism, or even worse. It was, after all, the US Smoots–Hawley Tariff Act of 1930 (an ill-considered protective tax levied against imports) which helped to bring about a contraction in world trade, which contributed in turn to the Great Depression. Years after the North American Free Trade Agreement, the United States regularly violates a number of its provisions, always employing various high-sounding rationalizations as protectionist fig leaves. For years, it would not import Mexico's single most important crop, avocados, based on some mumbo-jumbo about health. In fact, it was violating its own agreement in order to protect Californian growers, giving them additional time to adjust to competition. In the case of Canada, the USA has taken numerous high-handed, protectionist steps against products ranging from pork to lumber.

It is worth recalling the USA's response to the rise of Japan during the 1930s. A great many protective and some deliberately punitive bills were passed in Congress in an attempt to cripple the USA's new economic competitor, Japan. Some of these measures contributed ultimately to Japan altering its national strategies and led indirectly to Japan's attack on the United States. One would like to think that the USA has learned from past experiences, but there is little cause for confidence. Firstly, young Americans, reflecting the influence of what is known as the American Civic Religion, are generally not taught a balanced view of historical events. Secondly, the USA's reaction to the events of 11 September 2001 has been highly discouraging, almost predictably destructive and counter-productive, particularly the misguided and botched invasion and occupation of Iraq. An American response to China similar to its behaviour towards Japan in the 1930s would give cause for great concern in the years to come as it would be a terrible source of instability to result from globalization.

By contrast, the American government has in recent years taken a more accommodating attitude towards India, even recently agreeing to supply certain nuclear technology to a country which developed atomic weapons against the USA's wishes. There have been outbursts of anti-Indian activity, as with proposed legislation aimed at making Indian call centres less competitive by requiring Indians who answer the phone calls of Americans to identify their location and offer to transfer callers to an American call centre: a bizarre concept seemingly designed to appeal to the prejudices of ordinary Americans and to use those prejudices as a kind of trade barrier. United States legislators always disguise the meaning and intent of such legislation with formal titles referring to things such as "truth for consumers".

The more positive aspects of the USA's current behaviour towards India is based on several related facts. Firstly, the shelves and racks of American stores are not stuffed with Indian-made goods, as they are with Chinese-made goods. Secondly, India's economic growth rate has been strong recently but nothing like China's growth rate (roughly, 6–7 per cent for a relatively short time, as opposed to China's growth rate of 9–10 per cent for a much longer time), which has allowed China to increase both the quality and the quantity of its military resources. Thirdly, India and China have had an uneasy relationship for decades, and India stands as a potentially threatening presence to China. Some in the USA see India playing the sort of role that China once played under the Machiavellian guidance of Henry Kissinger, the former US Secretary of State under President

Nixon, in keeping the Soviet Union in check. Fourthly, some placatory initiative towards India became essential as the USA cosied up to Pakistan as part of its "War on Terror". Previously, the USA had acted punitively towards Pakistan when it became a nuclear power and a threat to India - such are the twists and turns of imperial policy.

The US government seems to have decided that China is the rising great power, ahead of India, and therefore its own key adversary, although there does appear to be some confusion on this point. A recent *Quadrennial Defense Review* described China as the greatest potential challenge to the US military and stressed its military build-up. On the other hand, John Negroponte, US Director of National Intelligence (and one of Bush's right-wing ideologues, not noted for his doveish qualities), said recently in an intelligence briefing to Congress that China's rise resembled that of democratic India, leaving out any reference to threats from China's military build-up. This may well reflect nothing more than a temporary wish, figuratively speaking, to keep another pot from coming to the boil at a time when so many others are boiling over, with US forces being pressed very hard in Iraq and Afghanistan.

In military matters, China has taken the USA by surprise on a number of occasions recently - and these kinds of surprises tend to make some quarters of the US political establishment irritable and uncomfortable. It is not clear, however, how much of this discomfort is based on credible analysis and how much on the kind of paranoid reaction which has characterized the USA's attitude towards Arabs since 9/11. There is also the distinct possibility of traces of anti-Asian prejudice which has a long history in the USA and in its policies. The USA's paranoid reaction to a number of events in the past - the rise of Japan, Communism, Islamic fundamentalism - reflect an arrogant imperial attitude of assumed easy superiority which does not welcome any clouds on the horizon.

China's explosion of a thermonuclear warhead not many years ago that proved through chemical analysis of atmospheric samples to resemble America's best at the time, the

W-88 warhead, lead to a McCarthy-like campaign to track down a betrayer of US secrets. Attention focused on a Chinese-American scientist at Los Alamos Laboratories, and the *New York Times*, undoubtedly prompted by the FBI, conducted a terrible campaign of innuendo. The FBI charged the man with a ridiculous number of things, a favorite technique of political police trying to get a plea on something, but the lack of any evidence saw him released with his career ended and his reputation ruined. It seems never to have occurred to the USA that China's new army of highly educated scientists and engineers could quite possibly have developed the technology in question themselves, or largely so, of course benefiting from bits and pieces of information garnered from researchers all over the world.

Chapter Five

The New Space Race

China has put a number of satellites into orbit, including a manned one, and has a very ambitious space program, including plans for landing people on the moon. The US military sees near-earth space as its most important base for the future "projection of power" over the planet. The USA's militarization of space is well under way, so China represents a potential challenge not yet posed by India. The great outcry from Republicans during President Clinton's administration about the remote possibility that China may have contributed secretly to a US election gave a heady whiff of the sorts of paranoid fears that lurk in some quarters of US society.

A short while ago, China launched a vehicle into space in order to destroy an obsolete Chinese weather satellite orbiting about 500 miles above the earth, roughly the same orbit as that of many of the USA's spy or global-positioning satellites. The test was apparently successful, and the message was clear: China is now capable of destroying the satellites which are the USA's eyes for war. The news was especially dramatic coming as it did not long after the USA admitted that a powerful Chinese laser, or some other directed-energy beam from the ground, had swept an American spy satellite over China, temporarily blinding it.

China's destruction of its obsolete weather satellite gave rise to a lot of noisy accusations of Chinese aggression and claims that China was militarizing space, but these claims are quite inaccurate. The USA, gradually and surreptitiously, has been militarizing space for many years. The space shuttle program, for example, has always been a military program; shuttles are, in fact, very costly and inefficient vehicles for science, and their use has sometimes even delayed the launch of important science projects.

America's military and spy satellites, many capabilities of which remain secret, are often used, if indirectly, as offensive weapons. Nations friendly to the USA are given priceless data to support their war and other efforts, while US opponents are left at a serious disadvantage. This was done, to give just two examples, in support of Iraq when it invaded Iran, and in support of Israel's assaults on Lebanon – both examples, by any sensible reckoning, of the USA using these sophisticated satellites not for defence, but in support of aggression which the USA regards as being in its own interests.

Perhaps, the clearest example of the militarization of space is the USA's anti-missile missile program, which has progressed beyond research to the deployment of actual weapons. No matter how ineffective the existing US system is – it has failed many tests, and independent scientists claim that the computer programming necessary for such a system is beyond our existing capacity – the fact that the USA is spending billions on its anti-missile screen, makes China and Russia uneasy. Many scientists and other experts warned some years back that a new US "Star Wars" program would start a new weapons race, and they were right. The Russians have already announced the development of a new warhead that spirals unpredictably when heading for its target and it may also put into service a mobile version of its highly-accurate Topple-M intercontinental missile.

China's response includes its ability to destroy the spy satellites needed as the "eyes" for such a system and an increase in the number and quality of its intercontinental missiles. China's DF-31A missile is its first solid-fueled inter-continental missile (these can be fired more quickly than existing liquid-fueled missiles) and it is the first Chinese intercontinental missile that can reach all parts of the United States. It could be made mobile, and a submarine-based version is currently under development. Up till now, China's nuclear deterrent has remained extremely modest, comprising about two dozen known missiles and the uncon-firmed existence of a small additional number.

China certainly succeeded in grabbing the USA's attention with its anti-satellite test, which provoked a strong reaction in Washington. But China's hoped for negotiations over the USA's anti-missile missile system have failed to materialize – certainly, China's immediate offer of negotiations towards a treaty against the militarization of space was ignored. America's stubbornly-held view of anti-missile defence is that it is part of its overall anti-terrorist effort, an argument which defies credibility especially in the light of plans to base some of these anti-missile missiles in former Soviet satellite states, in a way which directly confronts Russia. There has also been talk of American anti-missile missiles being placed in Afghanistan, as a way of combating Chinese ICBMs, again, a highly provocative idea, aiming to create uncertainty in China over the efficacy of its nuclear deterrent.

Another recent military surprise from China was the unveiling of the new Jian-10, swept-wing fighter. The project to develop this plane was apparently a closely kept secret, hence the surprise at its appearance. It is the same kind of fighter as the US F-16, the European Eurofighter Typhoon, or Russia's MIG-29, although its capabilities are not well understood. Whether or not it meets the performance standards of these other front-line, supersonic fighters, the plane represents a remarkable technical and manufacturing achievement by the Chinese, foreshadowing the day when

China is able to compete in building aircraft for civil aviation. China's current military philosophy of husbanding its resources and investing only in projects directly targeted at China's most important projected future needs has apparently enabled it to compete in the field of costly high-tech aviation which is open to only very few countries.

China's new investments in its military are, like so many things about China, strongly criticized by the US establishment. The truth is that they represent a small fraction of what the USA spends on its military, whichever form of accounting is used. Widely accepted, published data put China's military spending at about 10 per cent of the USA's, although some say it may be about 50 per cent higher than that as a result of hidden spending. Those estimates may be right, but they ignore the reality of a great deal of hidden spending in America, particularly when it comes to so-called black programs, and the unquestionable fact remains that America accounts for fully half of the entire planet's military spending.

China's recent military spending is driven to a considerable extent by what it sees as the USA's imperial attitudes and behaviour. Recall the incident of the US spy plane flying right up to the boundary of Chinese air space early in George W. Bush's administration and being forced down by the Chinese. This was an extremely provocative act on the part of the USA, similar to the flight of a US Air Force U-2 spy plane over the USSR just days before a scheduled summit between Eisenhower and Khruschev. During the first hours of this recent, smaller crisis, the new Bush administration took a hard-line approach, making no apologies (a Chinese pilot had died bringing the spy plane down) and demanding that the plane and its crew be returned immediately. After a while Bush relented, reportedly after having consulted his considerably more experienced father, and took a more accommodating approach. China then promptly allowed the crew to be flown home and returned the spy plane, after a bit of time, disassembled and in a crate, mimicking a much earlier US exploit, one that undoubtedly had provided many laughs over the years at the Pentagon. A defecting Soviet pilot had landed one of the USSR's most advanced fighters in Japan and the USA had returned his plane in a similar fashion. No one knows how successful the Chinese were in studying the spy plane's top-secret electronic gear, but generally such machines are destroyed by explosive devices detonated by the crew when crashing or being forced to land. Things can be learned even from demolished mechanisms. Then again, those devices don't always work.

China has not challenged American world leadership, nor has it set it as a goal to be able to do so, but this incident of the spy plane was interesting for a number of reasons, mainly in that it demonstrated China's willingness to confront the USA aggression in China's back yard. Had it come to shooting, China could not have won, but world public opinion was on China's side in what was clearly an incident of reckless behaviour on the part of the USA.

Few Americans appreciate the extent to which such high-risk behaviour characterized US activity during the Cold War. Intrusive US military flights over the Soviet Union in the 1950s were common. Indeed, Krushchev was irritated and angered by the extent of these flights which Eisenhower once observed would have initiated a war had the Russians flown similar sorties over US territory. There were also many confrontations between nuclear submarines, including a number of scrapes and collisions due to close approaches to Soviet boats. Indeed, it has been reported, and there is some evidence from photographs to suggest, that the advanced Russian submarine, *Kursk*, which sank during tests in 2000, condemning its crew to a slow death by suffocation, sank as a result of a torpedo fired in error by a US commander whose boat was closely observing the *Kursk*'s manoeuvres. If so, that incident might help to explain the kid-glove approach that the Bush administration has taken towards the Russians despite the history of belligerence between the USA and Russia, and the old Soviet Union.

The situation in Taiwan remains a smoldering fire that American conservatives never tire of stoking. Taiwan was confirmed as part of China in the international settlement of boundaries that followed the Second World War. Nixon and

Kissinger committed the United States to recognizing it as part of China. Yet independence-minded politicians in Taiwan, descendants of the Nationalist forces who lost China's civil war and sought refuge on the island, are regularly encouraged by US politicians, and American naval movements and exercises are a blunt reminder to the Chinese that it is not currently possible to invade Taiwan. China has exercised great patience in this matter, but recent provocations by the USA have tried that patience. Many of China's new weapons are geared to an assault on Taiwan should that island declare its independence. Most Chinese people view the USA's involvement with the status of Taiwan in the same sort of way that Americans would react to being told by China that Texas should be returned to Mexico. Since the USA fought its bloodiest war by far, the Civil War, over the issue of a state's right to leave the Union, it would be reasonable to expect greater understanding on the part of the USA, but this does not seem to be present.

Another irritating aspect of the US "empire" from the Chinese point of view is the USA's alliance with Japan, which US politicians regularly refer to as the "bedrock" of US policy in Asia. What few of these politicians understand, as they glibly utter these words, is that in recent years there has been a great deal of anger in China over Japan's behaviour during its occupation of parts of China during the 1930s and 1940s, especially on the part of the younger generation. Japanese wartime atrocities in China constituted truly appalling crimes against humanity. Japan has never offered an adequate apology for its behaviour, far less reparations, and Japanese history textbooks tend to skim over the period, which angers the Chinese. In China, the Second World War is known as the Anti-Japanese War, and, in the light of increasingly anxious attitudes in Japan towards China's current economic success, the Chinese would like to see Japan address its wartime record.

The USA could certainly avoid behaving provocatively, like an overweening imperial power, in China's own back yard. While the USA may have felt comfortable in past decades behaving in this way, knowing that China was relatively weak and incapable of offering any meaningful opposition, in future decades, this sort of US behaviour will carry the real risk of a war of some kind.

China would not need to engage directly in a war against the USA, which it knows it could not win in the foreseeable future. It has many, much more subtle options available for making life difficult for the world's current superpower. It could easily stoke resentment in various parts of the world against US interests, just as the Soviets once did. In extreme circumstances, it could even allow elements of its advanced military technologies, including those related to nuclear and ballistic missiles, to slip into the hands of spies representing interests hostile to US policy in various parts of the world. The US military is currently so over-committed that it would be reluctant to confront any fresh problem anywhere in the world.

There is absolutely no evidence that China wants any kind of conflict with the United States. In fact, China has been accommodating towards American policy in many instances, whether controlling the spread of dangerous technologies or assisting in reaching an accommodation with North Korea. For the last half century, China has not been involved in any aggressive wars, a time period in which the United States has fought dozens of minor and major wars.

China and India have an extraordinary endowment of human capital, and the era that we are now entering is one of applied intelligence. Never before have so many people earned their livings doing pure science and research, and the resulting torrent of discoveries and applications is changing almost everything in society, at an ever-increasing pace. The rise of women in Western economies reflects the underlying reality of great new demands for intelligent and educated people rather than scraping the bottom of the barrel of male talent. In the same sort of way, it is now becoming possible to utilise the immense human talents that have been locked up in Asia.

A global network, growing constantly in intelligence, reach, and adaptability, combined with the great intellectual resources of Asia, and a world hungry for better and faster devices and programs creates an almost unimaginable potential for change.

While there has been a good deal of hype around e-business, and one computer-industry bubble has collapsed, that collapse was no more than a cyclical dip in a long-term upward trend. The growing economies of the eighteenth and nineteenth centuries experienced a number of such financial bubbles, for example, the famous South Sea Bubble. It is not possible, looking ahead several decades, to exaggerate the possibilities of a world in which hundreds of millions of cheap and powerful personal computers (more powerful than those of today) are wired together providing equal access from any point on the globe. In everything from medicine to financial services and design and entertainment, new software for personal and corporate use and new Internet-based businesses are going to continue to change the way society does things, and at an increasing rate.

The demise of the conventional newspaper, printed and delivered to the reader's door is now within sight. So, too, is the demise of the conventional public library. Already, computers are encroaching on floorspace previously occupied by books. Already, on-line services and reference sites hold far more information, and are updated more frequently, than all the encyclopedias and books that once crowded library reference shelves. These changes will come in stages, rather than everyone everywhere dispensing with print at the same time, but come they will, and probably more quickly than we anticipate.

Imagine powerful, accurate translation services, specialized to deal with various technical or academic fields, available by subscription at any time on-line. Imagine financial management or engineering services of great sophistication instantly available in the same way, enabling even a smallscale builder in a rural village without a great deal of technical training to develop and test ideas on-site using a laptop. Or medical diagnostic programs as good as, or better than, most primary-care physicians, perhaps including laptop attachments to measure blood pressure and other vital signs. Any medical problems identified could then be referred to the best local hospital or clinic anywhere in the world, all of them having been listed and categorized on easily-accessible databases.

Imagine design programs in almost any field – fashion, for example – linked to computerized production plants in major markets around the world, producing new designs quickly with no transoceanic shipping involved. Indeed, with the emergence of truly sophisticated robots – the latest generation of Japanese robots already accurately mimic human activities such as walking and running – it will be possible one day to operate entire branch industries of almost any description from anywhere in the world – road work, building, chemical and nuclear plants, beauty salons, and armies.

These few notions, along with countless more, are not mere possibilities, they are certainties, coming in the not too distant future. The possibilities for economic growth and development and revolutionary social change out of all this are astonishing, limited only by our imagination.

I have been struck by the way in which Asian students in North America practically live out of their sophisticated notebook computers. They download and watch films; they download and listen to music; they do their homework; they play games with other people right across the planet; they communicate with their families. I have never seen a large group so comfortable with this technology, viewing it not as something that they have to adapt to, but as a natural part of life. United States investment bank, Morgan Stanley, says that while about 70 per cent of US Internet users are over the age of thirty, about 70 per cent of Chinese users are under thirty. When something is embraced to that extent by the young, it indicates that the next generation will develop a strong lifetime attachment. For the same reason, cigarette companies and fast-food chains used to aim, and when legal still do, most of their advertising at the young.

No one can accurately predict the future – and if one could, one would probably be cursed as Cassandra was in Greek mythology, to see but not be believed – but some things can be prophesied with a fair degree of certainty, and the decline of the US empire is one of these.

"What empire?" many will immediately ask. The USA, having been born in revolt against the world's great empire of the late eighteenth century, the British Empire, has always maintained the polite fiction that it is a nation dedicated to the highest principles of freedom and human rights, rather than an empire, which by definition would involve some form of rule over people without their consent. Americans, even in the twentieth century, have often shown considerable antipathy, and even contempt, towards old-world empires such as those of France or Britain, but many of them fail to recognize the reality of their own situation.

It is a fact that the USA has become a great imperial power. While there is no official recognition of this, such as the *et Ind Imp* that used to appear with the portrait of the monarch on British and Canadian coins, all evidence testifies to its truth. The fact of empire is reflected in America's fleets of aircraft carriers, its air and naval bases in many countries around the world, and an annual expenditure on the military roughly equal to the rest of the planet's expenditure. In no meaningful sense can such an aggressive posture be understood as national defence, despite the USA's insistence on calling its military the Department of Defense.

The fact of empire is reflected in the USA's innumerable colonial wars and interventions following the Second World War. The USA has toppled or attempted to topple the governments of many lands, including those with democratically elected governments, for the fault of disagreeing with US policy in their own neighborhood. The "American Empire" has generally opted not to rule its "colonies" directly, by appointing governors-general in the style of earlier empires. Instead, the USA works to ensure, by means of incentives and punitive measures, that local leaders or parties favourable to its policies rule in any country in which it has interests.

What is important to the USA is the safe and secure operation of its corporations and investments abroad. In principle, this is a legitimate goal for diplomacy and the giving of foreign aid, but the USA's bullying approach reflects the imperial reality. The USA which claims repeatedly to be a great defender and promoter of democracy and human rights, in fact, frequently works vigorously to undermine them. This contradiction reflects an inescapable, defining condition of empire: those over whom the empire rules simply do not enjoy the same rights and privileges as the empire's rulers do. This was clearly reflected in the old Soviet Union's relationship with its neighbours in Eastern Europe.

How is it, then, that an ostensibly democratic country can behave as an imperial power? We cannot help but see the contradiction of establishing democratic institutions for ourselves while denying genuine such institutions to others.

While none of the great empires in history have been run by a democracy, Britain was evolving into a great imperial power at exactly the same time as it was becoming a more democratic nation. The power of the British monarch was in decline as power shifted towards parliament, the once-restricted franchise was being extended, and all of this was happening while Britain was beginning to establish many of the great precedents, legally enshrined human rights and balances between different branches of government, copied in many modern democratic states. France's imperial ambitions reached their highest level after the French Revolution, and those imperial ambitions continued through many different governments and forms of the Republic right up until well after the Second World War. There appears to be no necessary contradiction between a country having a democratic government and behaving as an imperial power. Perhaps this would not be the case in a "pure" democracy, where the population votes directly on any major issue and especially when matters of war are concerned; but there are no such states in the world.

Western democratic governments tend to be governed by the principles of Edmund Burke, especially the principle that a legislator is elected to use his or her own best judgment, not simply to reflect whatever is popular at any given moment. Sadly, however, few legislators exercising their own judgment display the character, intelligence, and dedication to principle of Edmund Burke. Instead, in a government like that of the United States, legislators' every activity seems to be focused on obtaining funds for re-election, and these funds do not come from the bulk of their constituents, but from special interest groups. There is thus a divide between voters and their government, despite that government having been elected by the voters.

This divide is even greater where political practices are corrupt and the political environment is awash in financial contributions, as is the case in the USA. There have been many documented instances of electoral fraud in US politics. These include the well-known frauds in Illinois and Texas which helped to elect J. F. Kennedy, the fraud in Florida which helped to elect George W. Bush, more fraud in Florida and Ohio which helped to elect Bush for a second time, and the fraud in Texas which gave Lyndon Johnson his first term in Congress. Modern marketing principles have been proven to hold sway in democratic politics. Spending huge amounts on advertising, especially on the hypnotically-suggestive medium of television, offering voters incomplete, selective images, does get results much of the time. It's no different to selling soda pop, potato chips, or beer. Those in a position to provide the hundreds of millions of dollars for that advertising effectively retain the position of elites in the eighteenth century, a time when few people were allowed to vote. No other brief description could better capture the spirit and work-a-day reality of contemporary US national politics.

Chapter Six

Democracy in the USA

So, apart from the fact that democratic states are perfectly capable of acting in the same way as empires, it is unclear how the USA can claim to have a truly democractic and open system of government when the workings of its political apparatus are taken into account. One tends to judge how genuine a person's beliefs are from their behaviour; while Hitler may have delivered a stirring speech in support of peace prior to the Second World War, no one now accepts the proposition that Hitler was a man of peace.

But even if one does not accept the proposition that the nature of the USA's democracy is questionable, there is an aspect of the USA's behaviour towards the rest of the world that vitiates its concept of democracy in a larger sense. The USA's favourite slogan during its late-eighteenth century revolt against the British Empire was "No taxation without representation." The USA's revolutionary leaders strenuously repeated that expression in virtually every meeting and document. Today, the USA's electorate represents about 2 per cent of the world's population, and, of course, the other 98 per cent has no vote in US elections, and nor should they as far as the USA's internal affairs are concerned. However, where foreign affairs are concerned, US voters behave as a de facto world aristocracy. The USA's electorate, about half of whom typically vote in national elections with about half as many again actually deciding elections, is a very small segment of humanity to be deciding who should govern in dozens of other countries, who should be punished for straying from the dictates of US policy, and whether bombs should destroy the lives and homes of others.

Perhaps this helps to explain why US officials make so many speeches about democracy abroad while doing remarkably little in real terms to support it. Instead, they are often to be found working actively against it. In part, those officials are addressing their own citizens, offering reassurance about what they are doing and why, effectively advertising and marketing their activities as other than what they are.

Listening to the speeches of contemporary US diplomats in which they target selected countries – generally those which show signs of deviation from US policy, or, in the case of China, a country with which the USA runs an enormous trade imbalance – one might think democratic government is beyond evil and adheres to lofty principles, but experience teaches us that that is nonsense. Churchill was right when he said that democracy was the worst form of government . . . except for all the others.

Democracy is a method of government, not a state of grace. A nasty majority can tyrannize minorities virtually forever. Early political thinkers recognized this possibility and a bill or charter of rights was offered as the way to protect a minority against the tyranny of the majority. The USA adopted just such a bill of rights as part of its constitution, a very eloquent one, yet it has proceeded to tyrannize a large minority (actually a majority in some states) for generations, all the while completely ignoring its own Bill of Rights. It did this again and again, not only with regard to slaves, but also in its treatment of many other groups, such as the Hawaiian islanders.

The USA's embrace of double-think, particularly with regard to matters outside its borders, may well represent a common human frailty, but when a country enjoys such immense economic and military power, as the USA does, that common human frailty becomes a global problem. When the USA wants to detain and torture people, it uses an offshore location such as Guantanamo, Cuba, asserting that US norms, including the Bill of Rights, simply do not apply there. Most thoughtful people in the world would conclude that a nation truly dedicated to human rights would apply them outside its borders too. To do so consistently would be a far more powerful way to promote those principles than simply making speeches. Objective analysis can only conclude that the USA's practices outside its borders have far more to do with the maintenance of empire than with principle.

I can think of no better comparison for the USA's more brutal activities carried on abroad in the name of democratic values than France's activities in the wake of its revolution. French armies swarmed over Europe in the name of spreading revolutionary principles, many of which were worthy from the point of view of human rights and the advancement of human understanding, but such principles cannot be spread by bayonets. Soon France itself sank into the horrors of the Terror despite its enthusiastic embrace of *Liberté, Egalité, Fraternité,* and soon the tyrant Napoleon rose to power embracing those same words. The reasons offered for Napoleon's conquests and excesses were often the same ones offered for the first aggressive acts when true revolutionary fervour motivated many in France. Imperialism recognizes no form of government as its parent.

The US government, as we know from history, regularly interferes in the elections of other countries and makes secret payments to politicians and parties who favour its views, yet remember the weeks of indignation from Republican politicians during President Clinton's administration at the mere suggestion that China might have slipped money into a

US election. Such harrumphing befits the jowly faces of imperial privilege.

Once Americans loathed the idea of the kind of interventions they now rationalize as the USA defending itself, as though nations ever spend great resources on disinterestedly defending others. The old attitude was labelled *isolationism,* but there was more to that attitude than the slightly pejorative label connotes. Isolationism had the negative aspect of a refusal to have anything to do with international affairs, not just avoiding conflicts. The current US approach is not so much involvement as interference in the affairs of the world. Polls in developing countries today suggest that the USA's recent aggressive policies abroad have actually served to discredit the idea of democratic government as an ideal.

The views of those Americans who have come to be called "neocons" (neo-conservatives), a small group that has had considerable influence on recent American policy, contain an assumption – sometimes explicit, sometimes not – that because the USA is such a powerful empire, it should stop being timid about behaving as one and use its power to get what it wants in international arrangements. What the USA wants is deemed always to be worthy, more worthy, in fact, than what others may want in their own countries. Their attitude is a subtler, more refined version of what every imperialist in history has assumed.

For the most part, the USA has not fought the kinds of wars we associate with Julius Caesar or Napoleon or Hitler, although its bloody work in Vietnam and Iraq have sunk to exactly that level. The core of the American Empire was built by the conquest of places where population was sparse and the wars were small – its long march westwards over the aboriginal inhabitants of North America, in Mexico, the remnants of Spain's American empire, and, finally, Hawaii. Had these territories had large populations and been well established as modern states, able to offer strong opposition, the USA's growth during the nineteenth century would have more closely resembled Germany's bloody imperial ambitions during the first half of the twentieth century. It is not widely understood, including inside the USA, that there is no set of principles separating the ambitions and conquests of the USA and Germany – only time, scale, and ultimate success.

Once the greatest part of a "new" continent had been secured, practically boundless opportunities to exploit its natural resources, including what is perhaps the world's greatest stretch of prime agricultural land, existed. That attracted ambitious immigrants, frustrated and desperate in their overcrowded homelands, countries which had experienced structural changes in their populations during the Industrial Revolution, changes characterized by falling death rates and continued high birth rates, a phenomenon now known as the first phase of Demographic Transition, the general cause of human population explosions.

When death rates first start falling in any society, as they did in parts of Europe during the late eighteenth century – owing to advances like vaccination for smallpox, improvements in agricultural production and diet, and changes in sanitation – people at first continue to have the kinds of large families traditionally required to assure some surviving offspring in the face of a high childhood death toll that has marked all previous human experience. A continued high birth rate along with a decline in the death rate creates a bulge in population, a generation of people who have trouble establishing themselves in a society which has not made adequate provision for them (consider the huge expansion of schools and other facilities that governments in North America and other places undertook for the postwar baby boom in order to appreciate the impact on a simpler society undergoing rapid population growth). It is from this European "surplus" that the USA drew its early waves of immigrants. Once people learn to accept as a fact that the death rate truly has declined, that more of their children are surviving, they respond by having fewer children and bringing the high birth rate down. Thomas Malthus's famous, gloomy writing on population in England at the beginning of the nineteenth century was the product of his observing the early period of this transition, involving a phenomenon that he was unable at the time to comprehend completely.

Ultimately, the very size of the Empire of Liberty – a favourite phrase of Thomas Jefferson (owner in the course of his life of about two hundred slaves) which even in its day had far more to do with empire than liberty – was ultimately to provide US enterprises with economies of scale that few other lands could match. Ultimately it is not only size, but also the quantity of prime resources, factors of production and markets that matter. The USA's great belt of prime agricultural land stretching along the Ohio Valley into what is today called the Midwest, was well matched with immigrants who could not have hoped to own farms in their homelands, and who brought with them agricultural techniques and knowhow from a wide variety of places.

Proximity to markets is important, too, and despite America's distance from established markets, it grew rapidly with a young population living in a relatively healthy environment. The strength of the USA's pull on talented, economically desperate migrants from the Old World led to rapid developments in transport. The USA benefitted from fast-changing technology – increasingly efficient trans-Atlantic shipping, canals and railroads developed in waves over the course of a few decades – and population growth in the Old World created new demand for the output of the USA's young industries. In time, the USA's rapid growth built important markets for the whole world. Hitler's obsession with conquering Russia was based, in part, on his awareness of the long-term advantages which the USA's size gave to it.

North America provided an outlet for the population explosion in eighteenth- and nineteenth-century Europe. It was a beneficial relationship for both parties: rapidly growing parts of Europe peacefully disposed of excess population while North America gained skilled, ambitious people, technology transfers, and new market connections. Today's developing countries, experiencing their own population explosions, do not enjoy a comparable outlet for their surplus population. The blessings of inoculation and other health improvements coming from the developed world have lowered death rates in these lands while birth rates remain high. The rise of the USA depended on some fortuitous circumstances which have not been repeated for other nations. Timing, just as in the case of individual careers, is vitally important in the rise of any empire.

Over the long term of humanity's development, human migration has often proved an irresistible force, transforming landscapes and empires with a force equal to earthquakes and volcanoes. With the rapid growth of populations now underway in the developing world, that fact has long-term implications for many places in the world, especially the United States given the long border which it shares with Mexico. The US-Mexican border has already seen a lot of illegal migration, and a lot of resistance in the south-west of the USA (much of which, ironically, was taken from Mexico during the nineteenth century), an elaborate US programme of building cross-border branch plants (*maquiladoras*) for employment within the borders of Mexico (*maquiladoras* serve a double purpose, also providing US manufacturers with lower-cost factories not far from home), and the beginning of attempts by the USA literally to wall off Mexico.

The population pressure building today in many countries of the developing world, with no prospect of relief through migration, not only condemns those countries to unending poverty and underdevelopment, but could also generate mass migrations in some regions, bringing conflict and instability. This process can already be seen in some parts of Africa today.

China, of course, has its own severe population pressures, but, for now, internal migration as well as women's fertility is subject to the control of an authoritarian government. These two factors alone argue for the role of enlightened (with the stress very much on "enlightened") non-democratic government in the early stages of rapid economic development (though this approach is certainly not embraced by all those studying economic development). The great size of China's population and its level of education (China has a higher literacy rate than India, for example) gives it an important competitive advantage as labour can be substituted in virtually any quantity for capital, which China, like all developing countries, has in limited supply. As China continues to develop, however, it will face many difficult issues regarding the size of its population and internal migration.

Chapter Seven

The American Civic Religion

Most Americans believe, and are taught in school and through public celebrations to believe, that great waves of migrants have come to the shores of the USA in pursuit of the blessing of freedom. While not entirely untrue, this view is too simplistic to be accurate, yet this belief contributes to the imperial instincts of US society.

This belief has given rise to what critics call the American Civic Religion, so named because in its form and practices it goes well beyond what most people in the world would recognize as ordinary patriotism. The US Constitution and its Declaration of Independence are treated as this Civic Religion's holy writ, the Founding Fathers are its apostles, Benedict Arnold (an American general who went over to the British and planned to betray George Washington) its Judas, and its rites range from reciting the Pledge of Allegiance with outspread hand on heart to frequent, public outbursts of "God Bless America!"

There is an elaborate, and superstitious, code of behaviour towards the US flag, not dissimilar to the reverence with which the wine and wafers used in a Christian Mass are treated. These include not flying the flag at night, respectfully burning a faded or torn flag, and folding the flag in a prescribed way. It is quite possible that politicians in Washington have spent more time over the years discussing the many proposed amendments to the Constitution to ban flag-burning as a form of political protest than they have any aspect of human rights.

The USA's patriotic practices are blended with puritanical attitudes, and a certain self-righteous smugness also features heavily in the mix. In this way a number of superstitious, unsubstantiated notions become widely embraced. For example, the USA is a rich land because God favours it, other places cannot possibly be as free and blessed as America, and what America does must *ipso facto* reflect God's will. This kind of attitude plays a far more significant role in the USA's foreign policy than many international observers might expect in such an economically advanced country, and it is reflected both in legislators and in the ordinary people who vote for them. The whole set-up resembles a latter-day, quasi-democratic perversion of the old Church practice of granting to loyal princes in the fifteenth century the divine right to rule.

Dogma, whether religious or secular, is always a threat to clear thought and to human liberty. The US ideology and dogma of religious patriotism works in much the same way that the ideologies of former imperial powers did. It puts what should be civic, political decisions in a realm beyond honest and rational analysis, a place haunted by imperial mumbo-jumbo and governed by totems and taboos. The puritanical tendency to condemn all those who do not embrace the true faith and to proselytize the benighted is transmuted into a secular form which insists that people understand what a great place the USA is and demands that they follow certain key practices.

These beliefs certainly have significant economic consequences, at times causing the USA to misdirect a substantial portion of its national resources. The most dramatic recent example of this has been US activity following the attacks on the World Trade Center and other targets on 11 September 2001. A number of criminal acts, in which all the perpetrators died and which could have been prevented with the simplest security procedures which have long been advocated for other reasons (i.e., secure cabin doors and more rigorous inspections at airports), triggered the largely pointless expenditure of hundreds of billions of dollars on everything from complex travel restrictions to invasions of both Afghanistan and Iraq – a terrible waste of human and other resources. To gain some perspective on these enormous expenditures in relation to the actual size of the threat, consider that the number of Americans killed on 11 September 2001 is less than 6 per cent of the number of Americans killed each year on the nation's highways and less than 1 per cent of the number who die each year from cancer. The US reaction clearly bore no relationship to the actual threat and had more to do with a certain chest-thumping, wrath-of-god response.

There is also another perspective from which to view these enormous expenditures. The USA's establishment has used terror attacks, and the threat of them, as an excuse to further disenfranchise ordinary Americans, increasing the distance between most citizens and their government, increasing many citizens' sense of being humble villagers under the watchful eyes of an occupying imperial power in Washington, and further increasing the government's freedom of action in foreign affairs. The more closely one examines the character, attitudes, and connections of the people who have led the US war effort - people like Cheney, Rice, Rumsfeld, and Bush - the more one is convinced that this perspective is valid.

The US Civic Religion has the effect of whipping American foreign policy into a shape dictated by the fears and paranoia of a vicious domestic political environment. The late Governor George Wallace of Alabama, having lost an election early in his career, was quoted as saying that no one would ever "out-nigger" him again in a political campaign, and he was true to his word. Note the bizarre combination of open hate-speech with professed Christianity, for Wallace claimed to be a Christian, as virtually all Southerners do, including those who used to lynch people. A number of the USA's destructive interventions following the Second World War erupted at least in part from politicians fearful that their opponents would "out-commie" them. This was certainly the case for Lyndon Johnson foolishly committing to war in Vietnam – more than merely reversing his predecessor's policy of withdrawing thousands of military advisors – out of fear of political attacks from Richard Nixon. Americans of Nixon's persuasion frequently spoke in the 1950s and 1960s about China having been "lost" to the communists, and the accusation that other regions might be lost in the same way, if nonsense in terms of fact, was nevertheless a powerful political attack in a superstitious country. Of course, Johnson himself was not free of this belligerent, confused way of looking at the world.

The USA's Civic Religion and its propensity for puritanical attitudes played an important role in accommodating Cold War rhetoric and the associated decades of interference in the affairs of others, much as they do today with the Islamophobia that has to a considerable extent supplanted fear of communism. It is interesting to speculate about the role that the secular, pragmatic nature of Chinese society plays in that country's rise. Formal religion does not play anything like the same role in China that it does in the USA, where even non-church-goers subscribe to views that are clouded by religion, and this is not simply the result of restrictions imposed by a communist government. This relative lack of superstition could be regarded as a significant intellectual advantage which contributes to a strong focus on economic growth. Certainly there are superstitious beliefs in China – Feng Shui being an obvious example – but they do not present the same danger as US Christian fundamentalism which treats its opponents as evil enemies, to be converted or damned.

Many early immigrants to North America who participated in plantation slavery can hardly be regarded as lovers of freedom. Following the American Civil War – which was fought over a state's right to secede from the Union and not over slavery – and the constitutional abolition of slavery, the same people imposed another century of de facto bondage under segregation laws. The Abolitionist movement, a rather late development shortly before the Civil War, never characterized the prevailing American view until the North was sated with blood-fed hatred of the South after the war and came to demand the end of virtually every key institution of Southern life.

The many Puritans who came to America – sentimentalized in American popular culture as kindly Pilgrim Fathers wearing tall black hats, starched white collars, buckle shoes and praying over turkey dinners – were also hardly lovers of freedom, unless it was for themselves only. Mostly they were harsh and intolerant. They had fled Europe less because of religious intolerance, but because they had earned a reputation in many places for ruthlessness. Puritans had pillaged the great cathedrals of England following the Renaissance, smashing statues and windows and destroying paintings and ancient manuscripts. Some puritanical sects actually made it a practice to attend the church services of other Christians with whom they did not agree and raise hell to disturb their worship. The ferocious pamphlets and tracts written by many Puritans would today be condemned as items of hate-speech. When these Puritans arrived in the New World, they were among the most enthusiastic in slaughtering native Americans and supported laws and rules which were repugnant to those who did not share their beliefs.

The "American Dream", a modern political marketing term which is nevertheless widely embraced as truth, may well be shattered by the rise of China and India, and if that happens, the destruction of that chimera will prove devastating in the psyche of ordinary Americans. An increase in anger and hostility and a search for someone to blame are likely to result which would provide fertile ground for ambitious, unprincipled politicians to exploit. People outside the USA are generally not aware of how many angry people there are today on the streets of the USA. You have only to spend a short time there, not staying in a hotel in a tourist area, but living in a modest apartment and walking around, talking to people, to realize that the anger is palpable. It is an anger that is unfocused, but which can be attributed to a combination of decreasing job opportunities for the lower middle class, the decay of cities, a lack of compassion in a society taught to hate losers and the sheer hard work that is the lot of so many Americans. There is a huge sense of vulnerability in American society today which is not in keeping with its myths about itself.

The complete failure of current US foreign policy, and the inevitable backlash that will result for decades to come, will further fuel the anger of the American people and contribute to the bleakness of their outlook. Americans have also been deeply embarrassed during George W. Bush's time as president. The 9/11 attack on the Pentagon was a serious psychological blow, which explains the almost unbelievable speed with which it was restored and the existence of paranoid myths claiming that a plane never hit it. There is a painful sense of having been launched into another war and having almost certainly lost it, and this has happened at a time when joining a peacetime army is viewed as an effective, safe way to finance higher education. Many Americans are simply embarrassed by their president, but have little sense of what can be done within a system that seems impervious to change and throws up the same uninspiring choices of leaders time and again. Increasingly it seems that it is relatives of politicians (Bush, Gore, Clinton, Kennedy, Rockefeller, Romney, and many others) that are up for election, almost as though the USA were late-eighteenth-century France and the political class its nobility.

Despite some deliberate blurring with notions of freedoms and rights, the American Dream is essentially about economic opportunity, about becoming rich, at least by the standards of many countries. The USA's focus, to judge from its actions, has always been on economic opportunity and privilege, rather than on principles to do with human rights, regardless of what all the bad patriotic poems and flatulent Fourth of July speeches by congressmen have to say. The deliberate muddling of these two ideas – the freedom to become rich and freedom in terms of democracy and human rights - plays an important role in Americans' view of themselves and others. In the days of Nguyen Van Thieu's South Vietnam or Augusto Pinochet's Chile, dictatorships as totalitarian and brutal as those in any communist state, but with the supreme merit of letting capitalism rip, US politicians and media saw no contradiction in talking a great deal about freedom. Hundreds of thousands of naïve young men were sent off to the horrors of Vietnam with meaningless slogans about defending freedom ringing in their ears.

Especially over the long term, there are important connections between economic and political freedom, but they do not everywhere and always appear together. The early United States, despite the words of the Constitution and Bill of Rights, was not particularly free in political terms, and, in many respects, nor was it economically free. The early USA was ruled by a relatively small group of established oligarchs who limited very strictly the political participation of newcomers and the less wealthy. They also established and enforced many rules adverse to the economic interests of newcomers, and it has taken many years to strip away some of these. The American Revolution has been described - accurately - as a group of home-grown aristocrats taking over from a group of foreign-born aristocrats.

In the early USA, people could vote only if they were male, white, well into adulthood, and, importantly, owned what was at that time a substantial amount of property. In effect, an elite ruled the early USA, not very different in its basic characteristics from the elite which dominated the British parliament at that time. It has been estimated that about 1 per cent of the population of early Virginia was entitled to vote. The proportion of the population which held political power in the early USA was no larger than the proportion of the population which rules China today; the Communist Party has an estimated 60 million members out of a population of well over a billion.

For many of America's Founding Fathers, democracy was an unpleasant word, carrying connotations very similar to those which came to be associated with communism in the

1950s. This was true for Washington, Hamilton, Adams, Madison, Jefferson, and many others. They deliberately built many controls over the emergence of democracy into the structure of American government (Jefferson was not part of the Continental Congress which created the American Constitution, but his views were well known). The Electoral College – selected from a small pool of political elites – actually elected the president; they were not bound to respect the popular vote, which, in any case, was at that time anything but truly popular. The Senate was given significantly greater powers than the House of Representatives: the power to approve all treaties, all important presidential appointments, all legislation, and all Constitutional change. To this day few Americans know that the Senate remained an appointed body until the early twentieth century.

These facts raise two important points. Firstly, democracy is clearly not a necessary precondition for economic development. Many historical examples, not just the United States, illustrate this point. England underwent the Industrial Revolution and built a vast empire while enjoying limited democratic institutions and being governed by an elite. All contemporary advanced nations, including Japan, became democracies, or at least democratic, only after a considerable period of economic development.

Secondly, it is important to understand how the USA has developed into a more democratic nation since its establishment. The answer is that it did so in much the same way that virtually all nations have done.

All contemporary, poorly developed societies, as well as all early ones such as ancient Egypt or Babylon, may be roughly characterized as societies in which a small elite owns almost all the wealth and land, and a large, poor majority owns next to nothing. With steady economic growth in such countries, a middle class gradually develops, with its members having a significant investment in that country's rules and policies because they have businesses, homes, and savings. Through their accumulation of wealth, the middle class begins to influence the original elite, whose power derived from having inherited estates; the elite both seek the advice of the middle class and begin to be displaced in terms of power, privilege, and status. Generally, this happens gradually and peacefully, but sometimes eruptions of discontent in one or more groups lead to political revolutions. These revolutions seem always to have only a temporary impact because they fail to adjust the basic balance of power in society or they attempt to put some artificial substitute in place, such as a party claiming legitimacy over all others. Political revolutions, such as those which took place in France and Russia, eventually collapse, and the affected society reverts to the natural, more gradual movement towards democracy.

The first notable steps in the transition from the Middle Ages to the Modern Era saw an early class of merchants and professionals gradually brought into government as advisors, chancellors, members of parliament, and heads of agencies. Their success was important to national affairs, shifts in the economy were strengthening their influence compared with those who merely owned estates, and their voices could ultimately not be ignored by the monarch and great lords except at the high cost of arbitrary decisions. Any society in which democracy is developing will undergo a similar process, demonstrating an important, long-term connection between the economy and politics.

Contemporary India seems an interesting exception to this pattern, its democracy reflecting as it does values and ideas imparted under British rule, and its population remaining largely poor. Of course, India's democracy is far from perfect: it has frequently been manipulated, and its leaders do not come from the great mass of the population living at subsistence level. While India's middle class as a proportion of the country's entire population is small, in absolute terms it is fairly large, and certainly sufficiently large to sustain democratic interests. There is a parallel here with English as a language spoken in India. It is certainly true that most Indians do not speak English, yet the group that does is as large as the population of a substantial European country. There is a close correlation between middle-class status and speaking English in India. This developed over nearly two centuries of empire as Indians, endowed like the Chinese with considerable natural mathematical talent and entrepreneurial ability, served some of the needs of their occupiers, developing a merchant and professional class of their own whose services could simply not be supplanted by sufficient numbers of migrants from Britain, no matter how much the British establishment might have preferred migrants from Britain. In modern India it is almost as if there is a nation within a nation, an interesting and unusual situation.

This situation grants India an advantage over China in certain aspects of its development. For example, India has developed a huge call-centre business; customers in Canada or the USA calling a local company for help are seamlessly connected to English-speaking client service agents in India, often without being aware that they are speaking to someone on another continent. Indeed, the Indian employees have sometimes been trained in North American speech patterns. The number of English-speakers in India has also been an advantage for the large software industry that has developed. North American high-tech companies now often send a portion of their work on software to India. English is crucial for this work, although India's dated, colonial era speech patterns and vocabulary have created problems at times.

Financial services are another area of business in which India now leads China. To some extent this reflects India's former imperial connections with London, which remains Europe's financial services centre. Language also plays an important role here as English is the language of international finance owing to the dominance of New York and London. China has been handicapped to some extent in this area by its shortage of English skills in addition to the ideology and practices of communism. China is undoubtedly learning a great deal about financial practices through its ready-made laboratory, Hong Kong, which is still permitted to function in a number of respects as a semi-autonomous region, including retaining its own currency.

English has become a kind of de facto world language – at least for the time being. A remarkable number of Europeans, for example, speak fluent English as a second language. China recognizes this and is working hard to overcome what is currently perceived as something of a linguistic disadvantage (although the Chinese remain proud of their ancient language with its beautiful written characters and are supporting a growing number of centres abroad where Mandarin is taught). Large numbers of Chinese students, the sons and daughters of the new middle class, are studying abroad, not only in universities, but also in high schools where they are more likely to learn idiomatic English. Many private schools and Western universities are opening campuses in China, and they often include as part of their curriculum a period of study abroad. English is now also part of the curriculum in Chinese schools. Nevertheless, it would be a long-term project in any part of the world to train millions of people to speak another language fluently, particularly when a very small number of speakers of that language live in the country in question, as is the case with native English speakers in China. India is likely to retain its linguistic advantage in developing international services for a number of years yet.

In general, China may be said to have become the industrial workshop of the world while India has worked to become a great centre for international services. Neither of these, however, is likely to be an exclusive focus for either country in the future. Services are unlikely to provide much employment for India's huge, poor population, and China will certainly not be content to ignore the opportunity presented by the market for services.

Manufacturing industry is an excellent way to provide jobs for large numbers of people with limited skills, and all developed countries – owing to increasing international competition from many quarters, not just from China but between each other as countries recovered from the effects of the Second World War – have been moving manufacturing to progressively lower-cost jurisdictions. The USA has moved jobs first to the south of the country, then to Mexico and, most recently, to China over four decades.

Manufacturing has been an important path taken by all advanced countries in their economic development. As just one example of manufacturing's classical role in development, it has served to absorb excess population from the countryside, as young people left farms to do industrial jobs in the cities. This was a symbiotic relationship: as manufacturing produced more efficient tools for agriculture, fewer and fewer people were needed for farming, raising labour productivity in agriculture dramatically over time. In an underdeveloped country, agriculture employs most of the population, whereas in an advanced country, just a tiny percentage of the entire population (3–5 per cent) work on farms. In China at the beginning of its reforms in the 1970s, about 70 per cent of its population was engaged in agriculture while now the figure is closer to 50 per cent. Because manufacturing is many times more productive than agriculture in China, there will be a continued movement in that direction, gradually raising the productivity of agriculture and thereby contributing to national growth.

Services will continue to form an ever larger part of the international economy, just as they are growing sectors in developed economies, but it is unlikely that any nation would be able to rise dramatically from developing to developed status by means of service industries. This appears to be a fundamental weakness in India's position today. Were India to attempt to compete with Chinese manufacturing across a broad front, the resultant competition between the two giants would depress wages and costs and keep them low for a very long time to come.

United States politicians like to hector China over its lack of democracy, but this seems like a futile and counterproductive exercise. Why? In part because democracy cannot be established by a simple command. Democracy develops organically as a country's economy develops. The hectoring is counterproductive because the Chinese are sensitive about being told what to do; while they may listen politely to such speeches from Washington, they will leave such lectures feeling that they have been insulted. The Chinese are also sensitive to the general idea of exposing disagreements in public. The USA with its Puritan-derived inclination to shake its finger under the nose of anyone it regards as a transgressor is singularly ill-suited to to negotiating policy differences with the Chinese. These fundamentally different ways of thinking will undoubtedly contribute to abrasive situations in the decades to come.

There is no sound reason to suppose that China will not eventually develop into a democracy. Today at the local level there are already many democratic institutions and while democracy may develop more slowly than some would like, due to a strong Confucian support for authority among other factors, a kind of enlightened authoritarianism may well best serve China's development during the transition. A technocrat like President Hu Jintao, an engineer who worked on hydroelectric and water conservation projects, seems well suited to managing such a transition. The middle class that has grown so quickly in the last two decades is not always happy with the decisions of the Communist Party, but then neither are many middle-class Americans happy with their government at any given time. There is considerable leeway in China for discussion and argument about proposals, but once the authorities have made their decision, it is expected that that decision will be supported without further comment. China's new business elite do not discuss these matters in public or with outsiders, but it seems clear from discussions with young Chinese abroad, that this is the case, though they, too, are careful about what they say. This caution does not simply reflect the authoritarian nature of China's government, as many Americans may assume, but rather a more ancient culture, bred in the bone.

China has roughly three hundred family names shared by over a billion people, meaning that there are a great number of people with the surname Wong or Ma, for example. This emphasizes something peculiar to Chinese society, that it resembles in some respects a group of enormous extended families which share a set of long-established attitudes and beliefs. These shared attitudes are reinforced by much practice in getting along in extremely crowded places. China has roughly the same land area as Canada, including large deserts and many mountainous areas (about 80 per cent of China is mountainous). A sense of other people, due to the constant presence of others, has developed in the Chinese mind in a way which Westerners struggle to understand. When democracy does come to China, this characteristic is sure to work in its favour.

The political theorist, Daniel Bell, who teaches in China, among others, maintains that traditional liberal democracy may not provide the best model for China and other East Asian nations. Confucian traditions generally support the idea that there are natural elites or rulers in society, people who are intelligent, educated, and wise. This way of thinking tends to be alien to Westerners, although Plato expressed similar ideas on government. Christianity, too – Catholicism, especially – is coloured with this thinking. At any rate, China cannot accurately be described as a communist state today when two-thirds of its output comes from the market sector. Its government, too, represents more of a one-party, authoritarian government, being communist only in name after its many comprehensive reforms. There are some indications, if not dramatic, that the Chinese government is actually trying to identify more with Confucian tradition, but this may reflect little more than that it is seeking to replace its fading communist ideology with some new, acceptable, binding national ideology.

Chapter Eight

The Rise of the US Economy

The USA's rise to economic power occurred over a relatively short period in recent history. The Civil War (1861–65), which took place only about eighty years after the USA was founded, marked the nation's rise as an industrial power to rival Britain. The First World War marked the USA's real introduction to the world stage as well as the beginning of Britain's decline. The Second World War saw the British Empire fracture and begin to fall apart while the USA reached a level of influence in the world perhaps never known before by a single nation. The timeline of the USA's ascent demonstrates the extremely rapid rise of American power as well as the general significance of great wars as revolutionary events.

Some of the USA's economic success was due simply to the failure of other nations. At the end of the Second World War, all of its great competitors were exhausted and many had been laid waste. America had fought great battles, but, in relative terms, it had only just got fully going. The USA had not been bombed like Dresden or Tokyo or London. It had not experienced the unbelievable horrors of the war on the Eastern Front between Germany and Russia, with Russians piling frozen corpses like cordwood at Leningrad or the Battle of Stalingrad, quite possibly the most awful in all of history. United States deaths amounted to roughly half of one per cent of the approximately 50,000,000 who died in the war.

The USA, in high gear to fight a great war and relatively unscathed, easily became the world's largest supplier of many products. Even at this late stage in the USA's history, the role of a powerful government was fundamental. Immense military demands had swelled the capacity of numerous industries out of proportion to post-war domestic needs. The extraordinary opportunity that these humming factories presented for boosting exports helped the United States to make the very difficult transition of absorbing millions of demobilised soldiers back into the civilian economy. The USA's success after the Second World War was not simply the result of greater efficiency or unique know-how, despite a certain mystique surrounding US "can-do" spirit and manufacturing genius that grew and was elaborated on during this era. In fact, it soon became apparent, with the economic miracles of the rise of Germany and Japan, that others could do many things as well as, if not better than, the USA.

An important rebalancing of economic strengths and weaknesses is going on in the world at the moment, as is generally the case when a new power rises, and some of the changes are not in the USA's favour. The USA is certainly not about to disappear or to decline into puny insignificance, but its imperial power will decline markedly and its authority will begin to be questioned from several quarters. Moreover, Americans at home face the impact of new competition and are having to make the disturbing psychological adjustment that comes with seeing the USA's traditional dominance, which has long been taken for granted, battered. Over the next twenty to thirty years, we will see the face of a new world emerging.

The USA's decline as an imperial power will be due largely

to the rise of other vigorous powers, primarily China and India, whose special endowments of human capital and skills better suit the future demands of a global, electronic economy. It will also reflect other states emerging from relative economic insignificance - Korea, Brazil, and possibly Vietnam and Russia. The European Union is certainly a major economic force in the world, and could, with a shift of attitude, emerge as a far more influential power. The relative decline of US influence along with European interests may well serve as a catalyst to that end.

Economic growth and development should not be regarded as a zero-sum game (that is, where what one wins, the other loses), as that is certainly not the case. Increased trade creates more opportunity and wealth in total, but it also sets up many competitions that did not exist before. As time goes on there will be increasing competition for resources around the world. China, for example, has little crude oil, and the United States, once a great producer, has seen its production in serious decline for many years. In particular competitions, there is usually a winner and a loser; the repeated loss of battles will begin to breed in people a sense that they are losing the war. The coming great international competition for resources and other advantages abroad is unquestionably going to give a number of countries, including current, reluctant allies of the United States, opportunities which they have not enjoyed for decades for expressing resentment against the USA for past arrogant behaviour.

A recent meeting of the foreign ministers of China, India, and Russia probably foreshadows developments to come. Reportedly, many world issues were discussed but the most important topic was crude oil: India and China need to secure future supplies, and Russia is looking to diversify the markets for its crude production. Perhaps the topic of Iran was broached. Iran has the second largest reserves of crude oil in the world and is a good customer for Russian goods. It is also a pariah state in the eyes of Washington, making it a perfect candidate for closer commercial relations with India and China

Unlike economic development and trade, dominance - and

with it the privileges of empire – is a concept which is always defined relative to others; it is very much a zero-sum game.

The USA's imperial decline will also reflect internal weaknesses and the adjustments the USA must make in responding to many global developments. In a sense, the people of any wealthy nation, much like members of an old wealthy family, can come to glide on what was produced before them for a time. The children, grandchildren, and great-grandchildren of great entrepreneurial barons are often made of very different stuff from the family's founder, living off trust funds and pursuing political or other careers rather than creating new wealth. Most great families naturally slack off and decline in their influence and power largely for this reason. This happens with corporations, too. And while one should be cautious with extending analogies from the individual to the community, there are some truths here for nations, too.

The USA has been extremely flexible in dealing with changing economic circumstances since the Second World War, and the view of some observers is that it will continue to show great flexibility and resilience. People in the USA have become fairly used to frequent, disruptive economic change, as, for example, with the relocation of industries, first, decades ago, from old established areas like New York to areas in the USA's Sun Belt where taxes were lower and labour unions uncommon, and more recently, with the relocation of manufacturing to Mexico and China. During these changes, unionization in the USA has declined markedly, as have real wages, and old cities have been hollowed out leaving large derelict areas, but still the USA grows.

However, meaningful opportunities for young Americans without trades or professions have been declining steadily, and in coming years they will almost certainly decline even further. Fifty years ago a young school-leaver could expect to find a union job in some kind of industrial plant, which would usually have paid substantial wages and offered generous benefits (for example, US steelworkers used to get thirteen weeks of paid holidays after twenty years or so of service). This was the unskilled workers' share of the USA's privileged position as the supplier of just about everything to much of the world. But even by the 1970s this arrangement was beginning to crumble, and by 2000, it had largely disappeared. The limited skills of such young Americans were once protected from a considerable amount of competition by distance, but that is no longer the case. With unskilled labor, there is little an American can offer that a Chinese or Indian person cannot, except the expectation of a higher wage and better working conditions.

For a long time, the growth in US jobs has been in services, and the jobs associated with these are typically at, or slightly above, minimum wage with limited benefits. They are sometimes jokingly referred to as McJobs in reference to the gigantic hamburger chain. Americans have adjusted to these changes in many ways. In most families now both parents work, a development that goes very much against the grain of Puritan traditions and attitudes and which is often condemned by fundamentalists and some back-to-basics types. Americans, for decades, have been moving out of cities and even out of older, "first-ring" suburbs, in waves which radiate further and further outwards, to relatively cheap, low-density housing. In part, this is simply a response to the desire for more space and privacy, but it is also the result of an increasing inability to purchase space and privacy closer to the centre of cities. Many politically-motivated financial arrangements have assisted or subsidized these migrations, from making mortgage interest payments tax deductible to making mortgages available with virtually no down-payment to subsidized road-building and maintenance and the construction of parking lots and modest taxes on petrol. All of these subsidies and forms of assistance have been accompanied by a blind disregard for the environment, as typified by suburban garages with two or more enormous pick-up trucks or SUVs parked in them.

These kinds of subsidies and assistance cannot be endlessly replicated. In fact, even without intense new competition from abroad and the gradual disappearance of manufacturing jobs, some of these measures will probably have to be reversed. Quite apart from critical environmental considerations, the kind of urban sprawl in which most Americans live today is simply inefficient. Each far-flung little suburb needs its own police and fire department, library, hospital, and other services, and due to their size and the modest means of their residents, it is unlikely that the public services and facilities will be good. This pattern of urban development negates any possible benefit from economies of scale (in other words, a reduced unit cost as a result of an increased quantity of units). The possibilities for specialization, too, are largely lost: it is impossible to provide specialized police units, hospitals with up-to-date equipment, or high schools offering a large range of courses unless this is done on a regional basis. If, however, sprawling suburbia is to be supplied with these kinds of amenities on a regional basis, transportation and road-maintenance costs go up.

Much of the USA's urban sprawl has been enabled by cheap petrol. The real price of petrol (the cost price adjusted by subtracting past, accumulated general inflation in order to be able to compare the cost in different years effectively) in the USA has stayed fairly constant or even declined for decades. This is something that has changed dramatically only recently, and it is likely to continue changing as China and India make increased demands on world oil markets. The changing real price of oil has many implications. Americans will want to drive smaller cars and perhaps drive them shorter distance, too. There may be demand for cars which run on alternative fuels. The best products which fulfil these criteria are all currently manufactured outside the USA, where they were developed as a result of higher real prices for petrol caused by increased taxation.

If the USA were to make a sudden change in policy in just this one area, by, for example, substantially increasing the tax on petrol or outsize vehicles or by changing its national CAFE (Corporate Average Fuel Economy) standards meaningfully, it would induce great economic and social disruption. When the USA set its CAFE standards in the 1970s, responding to an oil embargo by Arab nations, it deliberately excluded light trucks and related vehicles such as vans because such vehicles were an important source of profit for US car manufacturers struggling in the face of more efficient competition from Japan. Today, virtually the entire US middle class drives fuel-inefficient vans, pick-up trucks, and sports utility vehicles. This is an immensely wasteful lifestyle – especially when one considers urban sprawl and the high cost of services as a result of all journeys, even the most trivial trip to buy a carton of milk or a newspaper, having to be made by car. It is not a lifestyle that is indefinitely sustainable.

Such a policy change would be a serious blow to the USA's domestic car industry (even today, General Motors and Ford are among the world's most troubled car manufacturers), but it would also be a tremendous blow to urban sprawl, which may be regarded with all its construction and associated activity as having become a major American industry over the past half century. Developing cheap farm land many miles from a city, quickly throwing up cheaply-built new homes, schools, and shopping centres while paving everything between has grown into a monstrous industry. Change in this area would be a huge blow to the USA's cherished culture of entitlement; an affordable suburban home is perhaps the single most important component of that culture. Very quickly, vast tracts of far-flung suburbia would lose their value and empty out in a kind of town planning equivalent of desertification.

But these changes are going to come about even without changes in government policy, when the price of oil rises sufficiently, and rise it will with the increasing demand implicit in the economic growth of China and India. The inability of many families to maintain their level of income will also contribute to this process, as will the removal, or decrease at least, of the many subsidies which now sustain the breakneck pace of suburban development.

This new challenge to the USA differs from past economic challenges. Firstly, it will come from several directions, and it will be in addition to the usual challenges associated with business cycles and technological change. Secondly, while the USA's new competitors will be battling to manage their rising fortunes that is a far easier challenge, psychologically speaking, than battling to manage decline. Again, economic growth by others is not a zero-sum game, but the American Dream and America's easy dominance abroad are fundamental to the average American's identity and sense of worth. Also, while economic growth is not a zero-sum game, that refers to a nation as a whole; any change in society, including war, results in winners and losers - some will prosper and some will lose out. A society only benefits from increased trade on average.

There are many Americans who talk about this or that aspect of moral decline as contributing ultimately towards America's national decline. This is not generally put in terms of the decline of empire since the average American does not regard the concept of empire having anything to do with his or her situation. Much of this talk of moral decline, by Christian fundamentalists or people like William Bennet, is conducted in terms of vaguely defined "family values" or "straying from Godliness." The appeal of this kind of talk is increased both by the social effects of economic change - increased divorce rates and more single-parent families, for example - and the very real fear that science is going to displace much of traditional belief. The appeal is further increased by the hopelessness of those in decayed cities or towns with no prospects. There are many areas of the USA, once prosperous city centres and neighbourhoods, that are as bleak and forlorn as anywhere in the developing world, or even Berlin after the Second World War. Their inhabitants have little incentive to move because they have no skills, and the USA is not a society that reaches out a helping hand. "Loser" is one of the most pejorative words in US society, and it is bandied around a great deal.

The USA's recent surge in Christian evangelical fundamentalism, not just as a religion but as a political movement, reflects this set of conditions. There is a powerful faction of religious Luddites feeding on fear and discontent. America has become the only advanced country in the world where the Biblical story of creation is taught in some schools alongside biological evolution. There is little danger that such superstition can banish the general hold of scientific culture in the USA, but these groups do play a political role as swing voters in many locations, and they are like a set of wild cards in a deck. The economic prosperity of the USA, or of any other country, can never erase every last dark pocket in society. The appeals that go down well with these Americans are unmistakably xenophobic and even fascist in nature.

While most of what is spouted about the USA's decline, whether evangelical or moralistic back-to-basics, is plainly nonsense from an intellectual point of view, and merely reflects fears about a rapidly changing world, there is a valid moral dimension to the decline of an empire's power, especially if one reflects on Gibbon's views on the Roman Empire or Shirer's views on the decline of the Nazi Reich.

Chapter Nine

Imperial Overreach?

The USA's current international situation is sometimes described as "imperial overreach"; some observers believe that it is trying to do so much that it is incapable of doing anything properly, and it is attempting to do things which it should not, out of an arrogant belief in its own power. This "overreach" reflects an indulgent, almost childish, way of relating to the world rather than an analytical approach – a luxury perhaps afforded only to the very wealthy or the not very bright. The arrogance of power often breeds enemies where previously none existed and is tremendously wasteful of resources. Take just one example, the invasion of Iraq, on which the USA has now spent several hundred billion dollars and achieved little beyond death and chaos and earned the resentment of millions. Given the argument put forward earlier about economic development leading to democracy, the USA may have done better simply to drop a portion of that amount in dollar bills rather than in the form of bombs.

That is, of course, an exaggeration intended to make a point, but it is not complete hyperbole.

In addition to waste associated with imperial overreach, the USA behaves selfishly with regard to foreign aid. The absolute amount given by the USA may seem large, but in terms of a percentage of GDP, the USA gives less than any other advanced country, and a generous portion of what it does give goes to serve geopolitical, imperial aims rather than to meet humanitarian needs or genuinely to promote democracy or assist with development.

Every nation needs some military forces, but in economic terms nothing is more wasteful of resources than the military. Producing large numbers of tanks and fighter planes which, for the most part, sit corroding and becoming obsolete from the day of their manufacture and keeping vast numbers of men under arms, expensively trained and equipped, but mostly sitting bored on bases, represents immense waste compared to alternate uses for the same resources.

Logic would say the USA should begin to tighten its imperial belt as the full force of new competition hits, but the temptation might well be to do just the opposite: to increase the size and quality of the armed forces against all new challengers. This would be a terrible mistake. It would replicate the thinking of the Cold War when the USA worked to defeat opponents whose very economic systems guaranteed their eventual decline. The great booming age of competition ahead will not be against nations who believe in junk science like Soviet ideology, but against nations who know just as well as the United States, if not better, how to create wealth.

Changes in technology, too, will tend to urge a reduction in forces. The USA's twelve aircraft carriers are an astronomical expense. They are a very material example of imperial overreach since they have little to do with the USA's defence and a great deal to do with "projecting power". Each carries a small air force of very costly planes, a crew of several thousand well-paid professional military personnel, and requires a fair-sized fleet to protect and supply it. The training invested in personnel alone on board each ship represents a true fortune. The carriers themselves cost billions of dollars each and billions more to run and maintain. But military technology is moving quickly, and it seems likely that before very long these mammoth ships will become sitting ducks for much more sophisticated missiles and torpedoes and perhaps energy or particle beams.

But stubborn people often refuse to accept changing reality. A new coalition of xenophobes, those with no job prospects, the hyper-patriotic, religious extremists, workers (including those in unions) afraid of foreign competition, the just-plain angry, suburbanites, and demagogic politicians could turn the USA sharply against the rise of China.

At first this may seem a fantastical thought, but a significant threat on the horizon for the next couple of decades is the US military assuming power in the USA. Since the 1950s and 1960s, this has been a periodic subject of US fiction and movies so it has been part of public consciousness for a while, perhaps originating largely out of the rise of what Eisenhower aptly called the military-industrial complex after the Second World War. We can see from the experience of the Bush government that Americans are not averse to having their freedoms restricted and even suppressed in the face of what can only be termed a relatively small and contained terror threat.

Wouldn't it represent a great irony if, at the same time as China was becoming more democratic, the USA were to move in the opposite direction? A possible scenario for this happening is not far-fetched, and an American general recently felt free to suggest that contingency plans exist for an emergency military-run government. The combination of continued fighting on several fronts in the "War on Terror", an additional significant act of terror within the USA, and perhaps a serious situation developing with China, most probably over Taiwan, could well tip things in that direction. While it is likely that any such event would be of a relatively short duration, a decade or so, it would still cause a great deal of trouble.

Whether it is through military government or an antagonistic civilian government, the most dangerous possible development over the next couple of decades would be for the USA to take a hostile and punitive attitude towards China and other rapidly developing nations. We have spent a lot of time reviewing American attitudes and history specifically to give readers a good feeling for why this is a real possibility, to better understand how and why US society might take this destructive turn. For those not directly hurt by past US policies and who believe the high-flown rhetoric of US officials to be sincere this is an important point to grasp. Our best hope is that the rest of the world will succeed in helping America to decline peacefully in the face of the rise of China and India.